INSIDE OUT DATING MAKEOVER

WHERE YOU CHOOSE, AND HE COMMITS!
THE UNCOMPROMISING, GROUNDBREAKING NEW BOOK THAT
TEACHES WOMEN HOW TO ATTRACT, MEET, AND KEEP THE
MOST AMAZING MAN OF THEIR DREAMS!!

KEVIN BOYLE

Copyright © 2022 by Kevin Boyle

All rights reserved. No part of this book may be reproduced, scanned, or distributed in any printed or electronic form without permission.

TABLE OF CONTENTS

Book Forward		5
Chapter 1:	I want you to have what I have.	12
Chapter 2:	Hire slow, fire FAST!	26
Chapter 3:	What every woman needs to know about dating, men, and relationships.	30
Chapter 4:	Biology – why men do what they do…	38
Chapter 5:	Are you worth waiting for?	44
Chapter 6:	Because most men live for the cookie.	50
Chapter 7:	But Kevin, he doesn't like Opera. This is NEVER going to work!	58
Chapter 8:	Understanding Men. Understanding The Hero's Journey.	62
Chapter 9:	It's time to change the rules of dating, where you choose, and he commits!	68
Chapter 10:	Self-Checkup, are you ready to date?	74
Chapter 11:	Are you the most amazing woman of his dreams?	76
Chapter 12:	Why does my six-year-old self have to ruin everything?	80
Chapter 13:	The Seven Steps to your Inside Out Dating Makeover.	90

Chapter 14:	Meeting; Where are all the good men?	98
Chapter 15:	Your ideal man is only one smile away!	106
Chapter 16:	Getting ready for your first date. The Ten Critical First Date Rules!	110
Chapter 17:	The Ten BEST first date questions!	114
Chapter 18:	Signs that he is a player…	118
Chapter 19:	After the date, your post date check-In.	122
Chapter 20:	Kevin, what are some basic rules for setting better boundaries and standards with men?	126
Chapter 21:	FAQ	128
Chapter 22:	The Ten questions you need to answer before having sex with a man.	142
Chapter 23:	Getting to Commitment; The FIVE Steps to Getting him to WANT to Commit! Activate your SUPERPOWER; Femininity!	144
Chapter 24:	Do you know how to be a challenge and how to be fun and flirty at the same time?	148
Chapter 25:	Do you have vulnerable, heartfelt conversations with your man?	160
Chapter 26:	Why men are afraid to commit.	166
Chapter 27:	Never stop being his girlfriend.	180
Chapter 28:	Life only gives you more of who you are being. Dating with an abundance mindset.	184
Bonus Chapter:	The one critically important life lesson that everyone needs to know.	200

BOOK FORWARD

"Gone are the days when a pretty girl can sit, hands politely folded on her lap, waiting for Mr. Right to come along and sweep her off her feet."

I recently found this article on dating and the challenges women face when meeting men.

I wanted to know how my thinking and methods compared to other thought leaders in this space, other dating experts, and other breakup coaches and relationship gurus.

As I read through the article and finally got to the bottom, I noticed the source. It was from an article in 1958 from McCall's Magazine, "129 ways to find a husband".

Ironically, 60 years later, many of today's modern women are still struggling with the same challenges of finding high-quality good men who are relationship and marriage-minded.

But who's fault is it anyway? Go to any social media platform, and you will see dozens and dozens of posts where men blame women and women blame men.

Hence, just one of the reasons I decided that I needed to write this book "Inside Out Dating Makeover, where you choose, and he commits!"

But, before we get started, **you need to strap on your seat belt** because this will be one wild ride. Most likely, you will feel very triggered by a lot that I am about to share with you because **this book is not exactly politically correct.**

This is not your ordinary "book about dating and relationships for women." Instead, it's real, "no holds barred" advice from a man's perspective.

No need to tell you that men and women look at dating, sex, and relationships VERY differently, and much of what I am about to share with you today may be quite challenging for you to hear.

But I believe there is a reason why you are reading this book. For any person to ever grow and change and to get what we say we want out of life.

We must always be **willing to challenge our beliefs, attitudes, and behaviors.**

This brings to mind an old saying; "You don't ask a fish how to catch a fish. You ask the fisherman."

You and I are going to look at it all.

I will challenge everything you think you know about men, women, dating, relationships, how you are showing up in your dating and love life and why you probably have been getting in your own way of having what you say you want.

So, the main question becomes, why?

In an age where women are more empowered than ever, and we have access to all this information on how to meet people and have better relationships.

Why is dating and relationships between men and women so messy and chaotic?

Well, you may not like the answer; we (as in both men and women) are all EQUALLY responsible.

It's because we are all a product of our upbringing, whether we like it or not.

How our parents treated us, how they made us feel about ourselves, how they modeled behavior and conflict resolution skills, **how society has conditioned us**, and our experiences with our peers, men, dating, and relationships dramatically influence who we are.

It affects who we see ourselves as worthy of and how we show up for ourselves and others in dating and relationships.

And we, both men and women, take this very messy, often damaged person out into the dating world, and we unwittingly hurt others.

Men damage women, and women damage men. And the cycle continues from generation to generation. Because no one tells us this, and not many people know what to do about it, and let's be completely honest, even when most people find out about it, most people do not want to do the "work."

And that includes both men and women.

The reality is, we all generally share some responsibility. **We all have our quirks, hidden wounds, and dysfunction** in relationships.

As hard as it is to say this, it must be said. As soon as you start blaming 'those guys over there' for your problems in life, that's the first sign that you may need to do the work. That's the first sign that you may not be taking full responsibility for who you are being in a relationship, how you communicate, your boundaries, your standards, and ultimately, your choices in men.

Because yes, it is not your fault if bad things happen to you in your life. No one can blame you for this, but it is your responsibility how you choose to react to it.

It is your responsibility to get the help that you need and heal your wounds from the past so you can ensure that you are not bringing any damage you might be carrying around into your next date or your next relationship.

And no one can blame you for not knowing this, I certainly didn't know. Not only did I not know about the work, but I also didn't understand that I needed to do the work.

I always thought I needed to date more and meet more people and that it would all work out one day. I was convinced it wasn't me that was the problem, **I was convinced** that it was women who were the problem.

I didn't realize that the person who was getting in my way of giving me what I said I wanted **was me**. Then, I realized that **no one has ever hurt me as much as I have hurt myself.**

Over time I learned this very critical lesson about life, that life rarely gives you what you want; **life only gives you MORE of who you are being.**

If you want something different, you have to work for it. You have to grow into it, and you have to understand that men and women approach dating VERY differently. You have to fight the good fight and win the most significant battle you will ever have, **which is the battle you are having right now with your ego.**

Life only gives you more of who you are currently being. This was a difficult concept to wrap my head around because I was the "nice" guy, the "good" guy, and I had the best intentions.

So, why couldn't I find a great woman to spend my life with? Quite honestly, I wasn't attracted to good or nice women (they are boring), and when I did find a high-quality woman (the ones I said I wanted), I either ended up sabotaging the relationship or pushing them away even though I hated being alone.

I was wounded from my upbringing and didn't even realize it.

And truth be told, I have resisted writing this book about relationships and dating for heterosexual women and men for a very long time. I don't see myself as a dating "guru" or even an expert, I never have, but I do see myself as a great dad, hence my reason for writing this book.

Clients from my Breakup to **THRIVING** Program in 30 days or less would keep coming back to me asking me for dating advice, and weeks, sometimes months later, they would report back to me, telling me that they had finally met the man of their dreams using my tools, techniques, and dating strategies.

My female clients, who had once struggled with dating and finding high-quality men, would tell me, "Kevin, I did not know that about men," "I didn't know how I could communicate better with men," and "I did not know what men are really looking for in a woman," Or that they had almost given up on ever finding a good man. And most of all, they would tell me that they found my advice life-changing and invaluable.

As my daughter continues getting closer to her teen years (she is 12 years old right now), I realized I needed to write this book.

It is needed because, as far as I know, there is no other dating book for women of all ages like this on the market.

Let's face it, most books for women and teens on dating and relationships are purposely written not to offend, because who in their right mind wants to upset their target market?

You don't sell a lot of books that way.

But if we sugar-coat things, is that really in the best interest of our daughters?

So, the vast number of books about men, relationships, and dating written to help women find a quality partner are telling teens and women of all ages what they want to hear, **not what they NEED to hear.**

And that's my dilemma. I do not want to be another man who "glosses" things over to you **about how things really are** because I don't want to take the risk of offending you.

I think, and I hope, that you will read this book with an open mind knowing that I only have the best of intentions for you and that I do sincerely want to help you find the kind of man you have always wanted.

In this book, **we are going to challenge many of your beliefs about men, dating, and relationships.** For example, the often-held belief that you should list everything you are looking for in a man in order to help you manifest the man of your dreams. Instead, you and I are going to take a deep dive into what I believe is **the most effective way possible** for a woman to attract, meet and keep the most AMAZING man of her dreams.

We are also going to challenge the long-held universal belief that women should take a passive role in dating and meeting men. In my experience, women who are bold, confident, and brave have a far better chance of getting the exact man that they want. And I am going to teach you everything you need to know to find that man with an easy-to-learn, easy-to-use method that you can start using tomorrow to meet the high-quality man you have always wanted.

We are also going to look at how to answer the question, "what are you looking for in a relationship?" and completely blow his mind! We will cover how to have conversations with men about commitment without scaring them away, the best places to find and meet high-quality men, how to protect yourself and your heart while dating, **and so much more.**

Having said that, we have a lot to cover, so let's buckle up!

CHAPTER 1:
I WANT YOU TO HAVE WHAT I HAVE.

INSIDE OUT DATING MAKEOVER

KEVIN BOYLE

I know a lot of single women who want to find a good man.

They're frustrated, disillusioned, **and a lot have simply checked out and given up**. I wrote this book to help women get to the root causes of why they are having problems attracting and keeping high-quality men and why their relationships are not working out.

My goal is to help women solve the puzzle of finding the most amazing man of their dreams, a man who will fully commit himself to you and who will want to spend the rest of his life with you.

I want to share with you exactly what I did to heal my life. What I did to heal the emptiness I was feeling inside and finally get off the roller coaster ride of endless serial dating, mixed and confusing messages, and long lonely nights and weekends spent alone.

Fast forward to today. I feel very blessed. I am a very happily married man and extremely proud father who has been in a long-term committed relationship to the love of my life for many years. Where both my wife and I love, respect, and cherish each other, and in today's world, I think that is quite the accomplishment.

And I want you to have what I have. While reading this book, I invite you to take the parts you like and ignore the parts you don't.

But I will tell you this. If you are willing to make some changes in how you show up for yourself and how you show up for men and you read this entire book, you will come away with a lot of very useful and very practical "aha moments" to help you with communicating, relating, and dating men.

And if you follow my simple and easy steps to attract and meet men, you can, and I believe you will have the most amazing man and relationship of your dreams!

The first thing I would like you to know about me is that I have been through it all. I have been lost, lonely, and confused. I have experienced marriage, divorce, and painful breakups, and I have experienced the wasteland and trials of modern online dating.

Secondly, I am madly in love with my wife. Magdalena is everything I want in a woman. She is my "dream girl." She is strong and independent. She and I are true equals in our relationship and our marriage, and I know she respects me as a man and as her husband.

Magdalena is playful, fun, flirty, and very sexy. She has a full-time job, and she knows how to appeal to the man in me. Once I met her, I knew that I wanted to be with her, and only her, and now 11 years later, we are happily married, still passionately in love, and blessed with a wonderful daughter who every year is recognized for leadership and service to others at her school.

My daughter Chiara is a lovely, intelligent, and very perceptive 12-year-old. My daughter and I are very close, we talk about a lot of things, and it was then that the idea for the book "The Inside Out Dating Makeover, Where You Choose, and He Commits" was born.

As she starts to enter her teenage years, I want to assure you the advice I am going to give you will be the same advice I will give her. In fact, truth be told, **this book was written specifically with my daughter in mind.**

So, you might be asking, Kevin, when should I introduce this book to my teenage daughter? Because yes, I have written this book for women of all ages, but I do realize that some of the topics (like sex and flirting) can be quite daunting!

As in all things family-related, it is up to you when you feel the most comfortable, but I have a question, would you rather your daughter be having these conversations with you or their friends at school?

Because guess what is the **number one reason** why teenage girls decide to have sex?

According to a study by the Department of Health, **seventy-six percent** of young girls said that they and their friends have sex primarily because they want to **please their boyfriends.**

And in a poll conducted by Seventeen magazine and the Ms. Foundation, they found in a survey of one thousand 13- to 21-year-olds that an overwhelming 81 percent of girls who had already had sex **wished they'd waited** until they were older.

So, I think our kids need us. They need our guidance during what can be a very confusing time in their lives.

I always suggest starting off with very light conversations about what is going on at their school. Are any of their friends "boy or girl crazy"? What do they think about that? If you can take the focus off of them and make your conversations more general, it can often help get them to open up about what they are thinking and experiencing.

Then when you feel that they are ready and you are ready, introduce this book to your daughter.

Because she needs to know that becoming sexually active and losing your virginity is a big step in a young person's life. It's not something you can ever get back. You can't just have casual sex, wake up the next day, realize it was a huge mistake, and pretend it never happened.

A question I often get from clients is, well then, Kevin, how long do you think I should wait until I have sex with a man?

It depends on how old you are, what stage of life you are in, and what your goals in dating are. Overall, I think young people should wait until they are at least 18, **if not older,** before becoming sexually active because, in my opinion, both young women and young men should give themselves more time to experience life and mature.

Being sexually active can either be one of the best, most wonderful experiences of your life, or it can be one of the biggest regrets of your life.

Because once you have done it, once you have lost your virginity, in order not to feel bad about yourself, you convince yourself and your peers it's ok, that it does not affect you, you go out, and you do it again. You get your highs, and you get a lot of lows, and you start to wonder if the lows are worth it.

Because waiting for the "right" man is not just about protecting your heart, and it's not just about the risk of pregnancy or worrying about getting an STD. It's more about **protecting your emotional and physical well-being.**

Regarding sexual intimacy, 20% of young women experience some type of violence or aggression from young men. It is more common today for boys and young men to take their ques from readily available porn, modeling aggressive performance-type sex rather than focusing on experiencing genuine intimacy and connection with their partner.

And this can put a young woman in a very dangerous and vulnerable position.

Therefore, in my opinion, it's not about losing your virginity per se, it's about who you choose to lose it with and when.

So, if you are feeling pressured by him, pressured by your peers, if you are feeling lonely, if you are using sex to fill an emptiness inside of you, or to help you keep a guy or make him happy, then I would say **DON'T do it.** (More about how to say no to men on page 126 of the FAQ).

The number one problem I see in women of all ages when it comes to men, dating and relationships are that most people are so focused on finding the right person **because they are so lonely**, or feeling so empty inside, that they completely forget about what it takes to **BE the right person.**

And the "right" person is not someone who does something because they want to please others.

Teenagers should be focused on school, getting good grades, making friends, engaging in social activities, and given time to mature and learn how to set boundaries and why boundaries and standards are so important in life and in relationships.

But more importantly, before making such huge life-changing decisions, teens need to learn this one life skill that will take care of them for the rest of their lives.

Is what I am about to do, **protect and align with my best long-term interests?**

I want my daughter Chiara to succeed in dating, in relationships, in life, and in meeting a high-quality man who would make a fantastic husband and father, a man who will love, cherish, respect, and devote his life to her and their relationship.

And lastly, I do not believe that the most popular dating and relationship books available today give our kids the best advice about what is really important in dating and what they should focus on.

The relationship that we have with ourselves. Do we respect ourselves enough to say no to another person when they or our friends make us feel uncomfortable or pressured into doing something we might not want to do?

So, I decided I had to write the book myself.

Just to give you one example, some of today's most prominent dating gurus and so-called experts in the industry actually advise women on how to respond to sexually inappropriate texts or direct messages from men.

This is terrible advice to be giving any woman of any age, and I am shocked they would ever give it.

Ladies, there is only one appropriate response to a man or a boy who sends you a text that says, "Heyyyy girl, super sexy photos, you are so beautiful, can you send me more?" or sends you a picture of his privates.

The proper and only response is BLOCK.

There is nothing to say. There is no reason to engage with this person, and you will never educate or correct him if his parents did not raise him right.

Dating experts and modern-day relationship gurus will tell you when you should or shouldn't have sex with a man. Some will recommend the 3-date rule, while others suggest the 3-month rule. All are well-intentioned, but again very bad advice.

Anyone who uses time as an arbitrary number to determine when they should or shouldn't have sex with someone is getting it all wrong, with one exception.

Teenagers.

In the same government-funded study done by the Department of Health, which I cited earlier, they found that young women who had sex before 17 years of age were **almost 70 percent more likely** to **experience an unwanted pregnancy.** They were also three times more likely to experience abortion in their lifetime than those who waited until they were older.

My advice to young women is always the same. No matter what anyone else says or tells you, **there is only one first time**, so why not wait until you are emotionally ready and when you can share it with someone special?

To that end, regardless of your age, I do have a list of 10 questions you should be asking yourself later on in the book before deciding to be intimate with a man. (Found on page 143).

Because as a woman, you need to know this very important life lesson.

You need to respect yourself first before you can ever expect a man or anyone else to respect you.

You need to have STRONG, solid boundaries because when you do, the way men treat you, their expectations of the date, and the relationship changes.

When you are grounded in who you are being and confident in who you are, your boundaries will inherently become part of you.

Over time, you will learn that not all people that you meet are what they pretend or appear to be and that if you **put your trust in the wrong people** enough times, **it will damage you.** Over time, this damage affects how you show up and how you see and experience men.

My original book, "From Breakup to THRIVING in 30 Days or Less," talks about and **teaches women how to show up for themselves first** before they ever show up for a man.

The book goes into great detail on how to change your experience with men and how they experience you by being 100% grounded in who you are being, having solid boundaries, and by doing the work.

Know that when you do the work, when you heal your wounds from the past when you heal and let go of any and all disempowering limiting beliefs and unhealthy relationship patterns that you might have, the way you show up in your dating and your love life changes. The way you communicate with your partner changes, and the way your partners treat you changes.

And this is the best part! Your EXPERIENCE with dating, relationships, and with the opposite sex CHANGES because their experience of you changes!

After taking my advice and implementing the core concepts in my original book, my clients are finding, attracting, and entering into relationships with the most amazing high-quality men of their dreams!

But before we get started on dating tips and strategies, I have a question for you. Have you ever played chess?

If not, are you familiar with the concept of chess?

Have you ever wondered why a game created over 1400 years ago in an age of patriarchy where men dominated women in almost every aspect of society, a game created by men and played primarily by men, **why the single most powerful piece in the game is the Queen?**

Have you ever wondered why every single piece on the board is male except the Queen?

I believe it's because men have always recognized how truly powerful, complementary, and how special women are.

Women help keep our society strong when they make good choices in men who will be good fathers to their children. Women help keep our society strong when they ensure their children grow up in loving, intact families with men who want to be fathers.

So, I wrote this book because I wanted to remind modern women and I wanted women to rediscover what all-powerful women have known since the dawn of time.

That beside every great man is a great woman. Not ahead, not behind, but beside.

Because unfortunately far too many of us have forgotten the lessons of history, and we have, as a society adopted many distorted views, beliefs, and attitudes toward both men and women.

For example, did you know that the average everyday man had to win the right to vote just like women?

That prior to 1876 in the vast majority of cases the only people who could vote were wealthy landowners and the powerful elite.

In fact, middle and lower-class men did not win the right to vote until 1876, only 36 years before women won the right to vote.

And that after winning the right to vote, good men in turn helped women fight for the right for women to vote through the suffrage movement in 1920.

Meaning, both common everyday men and women have always been oppressed by the political elites and the rich and powerful.

Go watch a movie or read a book about World War 1. In the trenches with the men would be an officer with a whistle and a pistol. When he blew that whistle, the men went over the trench walls, and they would charge into the enemy's machine guns.

Most men never made it. Most men died.

And if you refused to go over that wall and charge into the machine gun nest?

Punishments for disobeying orders were severe, and men who were convicted of "cowardice in the face of the enemy" or desertion from their unit could either be court martialled and sentenced to hard labour, receive a death sentence, or in some armies the officers would simply shoot you out in the field.

That was the political elite, oppressing men.

Know that our fight is not with each other. It is, and it has always been with the political, corporate, and the rich and powerful elite who dictate the rules and the norms by which we live by.

That life has always been very difficult for both men and women. That as far as up until the nineteenth century, peasants, comprising both men and women accounted for 78 percent of the total population and the vast majority of people lived in abject poverty.

The vast majority of men and women had very few rights, and if you were a serf, you were the poorest of the peasant class. Man or woman, you were basically a slave. Lords (the noble class) owned the serfs who worked the lands.

And that when men and women came back from the Afghanistan war, one in five veterans suffered from PTSD. Depression, loneliness, anxiety, insomnia, homelessness, and increased suicide rates.

How can we say that the powerful and the elite or even our society as a whole cares about our veterans when one tomahawk missile costs 1.87 million dollars, and our veterans are out living on the street with PTSD?

When you can look at things objectively and set aside the narrative that others have wanted you to adopt - which is to blame our problems on the opposite sex, you will come to realize a great truth.

The rich and powerful, the elites of our society oppress both men and women equally. That we are all in this together.

That we need to come together, and we need to realize the importance of strong, intact, loving, and supportive families.

That men and women are **complementary** in their roles in families. Just as in the chess pieces on the board, they both bring very different and necessary strengths to the table.

The feminine and the masculine.

And it's this very reason why **we need each other.**

Just as most women are looking for a man who is comfortable in his masculinity, most men are looking for women who are comfortable in their femininity.

To be clear, I do not see gender roles as being static or absolute, I see the masculine and the feminine as fluid. There is a certain ebb and flow in successful relationships. But keep in mind this book is about heterosexual male and female dating and attraction preferences, so I will be speaking in very general terms throughout the book.

Because there is great power in a woman who fully embraces her femininity.

And if you are not comfortable being feminine, I want you to ask yourself, why?

Yes, masculine traits will get you what you want at work, it will help you make more money, it will help you get more recognition at work, and it may even help you get a promotion.

But, ask any man, and he will tell you. When a woman fully embraces her femininity around a man. He becomes putty in her hands, he melts, he becomes powerless around her, and he will do anything to provide for her and protect her.

Just ask any man's daughter.

And the father-daughter relationship fulfills one more aspect of what truly brings out the best in a man.

A daughter looks to her father for leadership.

That is when a man is at his best. That is when a man lives up to his true potential. When a man embodies these three characteristics; Provider, protector, and as a leader. This is when a man truly inspires those around him.

Because it allows him to show up as the hero.

Not all wives know how to let their men show up as heroes, but their daughters do.

Ask any man, and they will tell you that a woman's superpower comes from her femininity.

Masculine and feminine **are not** about you being submissive to men.

Being feminine is not about taking a back seat to men, pretending you are weak, or diminishing yourself for a man to help preserve his ego.

Most men today believe in equality, in sharing household responsibilities, and most men believe that women deserve equal pay and an equal say in the relationship.

The type of femininity I am talking about is the type where you allow space for your man to show up for you as your hero.

When you are feminine with your man, you can and will get whatever you want, and most importantly, your femininity will get you the relationship with the man that you want. A man who wants to love you, cherish you and fully commit himself to you.

CHAPTER 2:
HIRE SLOW, FIRE FAST!

INSIDE OUT DATING MAKEOVER

KEVIN BOYLE

When I start working with women, and we start talking about men, women, dating, and relationships, I always ask, what do you believe is the key to success in business?

Business? Kevin, what does business success have to do with relationships and finding a high-quality man who is marriage and family-minded?

Everything.

So, stay with me while I explain.

One of the key ingredients to success in business and relationships is the people you hire and the people you choose to surround yourself with.

Are they the right people? Do they treat you with respect? Do they consult with you when a decision needs to be made? Are they available when you need them?

The key mantra in business is this; **hire slow, and fire fast.**

Why is this? Because one bad employee can ruin your business.

Just like marrying the wrong man can ruin your life.

In addition, when you hire a marketing director, do you unwittingly undermine them by doing their job? I hope not.

Men want you to be feminine around them, just like you probably like and want your man to be masculine around you.

But there's another reason. It's about leadership and **men wanting to be your hero.** And a man wanting to be your hero, or hold open the door for you, is not a bad thing. It's not about diminishing you or saying you can't do it for yourself.

It's about a man wanting to show up as the best version of himself. A man who is considerate and respectful towards others.

Just like you want the freedom to show up in a way that honors who you are as a woman.

So, the question becomes, can you allow room for your man to show up as your hero without feeling like you have to give up a part of yourself in order to do so?

I want you to know that men can be masculine without being toxic, aggressive, or violent.

That although it is wise not to trust all "men," you should be able to trust "your" man, and if you don't, you might, for the sake of your children and the sake of your marriage, take a look at that.

Dress for the job you want, not the job you have.

Because both men and women, when dating, have to ask themselves. Am I offering the right product or service to the market? Something the market has identified that they want?

In other words, are you what men want? If you are serious about wanting a long-term committed relationship with a man, you need to know it's not just about what you want from a man or a relationship. It's also important to consider what he wants from a woman and a relationship.

Because, yes, your packaging might be prettier and more visually appealing, so yes, you are offering what the market says it wants. And yes, your "packaging" will get you the man, but it is not what is going to get him to stick around. So, you need to be 100% honest with yourself in knowing what the customer's experience is like after they open the box or start using your service.

Because this is what will truly separate you from anyone else he has ever dated or is considering dating.

You need to ask this one critically important question of yourself like you would if you were starting a new business.

What are you willing to do that your competition is not?

Because here's the secret, if you are serious about meeting the most amazing man of your dreams. Why not consider being the most incredible woman of his dreams?

BOLD, confident, and BRAVE!

Just like you are a badass in business or at your job, why can't you rewrite "The Rules" and be a badass when it comes meeting and attracting the love of your life?

I believe you should strongly consider being willing to be more proactive in your dating life and start going after what it is that you say you truly want.

Because I do believe women have a better innate intuition than men do, and I do think it makes more sense for women to do the "choosing."

But there are other things you need to consider as well.

Are you willing to question who you are being and **what wounds you have been dragging** from your past into your relationships?

Are you willing to question your attitude towards men, your fears when it comes to men and relationships, your insecurities, your distrust towards men, and your defensiveness?

And lastly and most importantly, are you willing to do what the vast majority of women are unwilling to do to finally attract and keep the most amazing high-quality man of your dreams?

Because if you are, then read on!

CHAPTER 3:
WHAT EVERY WOMAN NEEDS TO KNOW ABOUT DATING, MEN, AND RELATIONSHIPS.

INSIDE OUT DATING MAKEOVER

KEVIN BOYLE

As a young woman, should you wait to have sex with a man, even in this modern age of promiscuity, hookup culture, online dating, "hanging out," social media, and the age of the empowered woman?

Before I answer, you need to know this about me. I married a strong independent woman, I believe strongly in equality, and most importantly, I want my daughter to know that she can be and do anything that she sets her mind to.

I am pro-woman, pro-man, and most importantly, **pro-family**, and I want to be crystal clear in my message to you.

I believe dating in today's society is very messy and chaotic for both men and women, but more for women in particular.

Why?

Because mother nature is very cruel in her design.

If you take anything from this book, I hope you can understand this fundamental "truth" about the differences between men and women.

At 18 years old, men hold very little value to a woman in terms of what she generally is looking for in a marriage partner, which is a man who can create resources and provide for his family alongside her.

A boy who hopes to be a man must invest in himself, his education, and his character, and he needs time to build those resources, become more mature, become more confident, and, over time, become a "man."

In fact, when I give young men dating advice, I tell them to go to a gym, work out, do the work and heal your wounds, learn how to make money, find purpose and meaning in your life, have a strong masculine frame, and then be patient.

Your time will come.

I ran into a very interesting fact the other day. Did you know that most women's brains become fully developed at 22, while most men's brains do not develop fully until they reach 30?

This is why in my opinion, most men do not really evolve into the "best versions" of themselves until they are in their early 30s.

While the experience for women is directly the opposite, between the ages of 20 to 30 years of age, a woman is at her highest value **for a man looking to marry and start a family.**

This is why in my opinion, **women need to mature much faster than men**. They have to because so much is riding on a woman's ability to make good decisions regarding who she dates, who she chooses as a life partner, and who she chooses to father her children.

Studies conclusively show that most men prefer women who are younger than them.

There are a variety of reasons for this; sexual desirability, fertility if he desires children, and lastly, younger women generally tend to be more agreeable and easier to be with than older, more established women. This is because a younger woman tends to look to an older man not just for resources but also for protection and guidance.

Thus, enabling a man to fully fulfill his desired role in a relationship as a provider, a leader, and a protector.

While women, generally, are looking for a lot more from a man. Confidence, charisma, intelligence, strength, competence, an established career, a good social network, etc. It's very difficult for younger men to have all of these qualities in place. It's why women generally prefer older, more mature men.

As you can see, a man must earn his value, which takes time. A woman grows up already having high value to men. She has been socialized in this regard. It becomes part of her identity. So, her belief system becomes. I have value. Men throw themselves and their resources at me.

This leads women to the false belief that as long as she maintains good looks and figure, this attention from men will last forever.

And this is a woman's **greatest folly and greatest challenge.**

Most women want to have the right and the opportunity to dive deep into their studies, their careers, to be able to explore the world and its adventures, as well as have fun and meet interesting new people before they even think about getting married and having children, and rightly so!

But this is where the dating environment can be extremely challenging for a talented, successful, career-oriented woman.

For women, the fact that their bodies have a ticking biological clock is **a painful, inescapable truth.**

Know that women **who do not prioritize relationships and picking the right man through their 20s** will be asking where are all the good men in their 30s, 40s, and 50s?

In this regard, mother nature and men's dating preferences are very cruel to women.

Because as a woman grows older, her intrinsic value increases. She advances in her career, makes a lot more money, has more status in her community, is more confident, and is much more mature and self-assured.

But all of this self-improvement comes at a cost, and it's during this time that the doors to dating men slowly begin to close.

A recent study from the University of British Columbia in Canada on female dating preferences shows that 93% of women prefer to date "up."

The higher up the status ladder a woman climbs, the fewer men she will see as a desirable mate. And as she continues to succeed in her job or career, her options for a mate start getting smaller and smaller.

It's called hypergamy.

Leading to a very interesting and frustrating dynamic for women.

As mentioned earlier, over time, a male's value to the opposite sex increases as he gathers more resources and more status, and more doors open up for him to women to date as he becomes more competent, while as a woman, as she gets older, her value decreases to a marriage-minded man and her options for finding suitable mates are getting less and less as she experiences more and more success in her career.

And then it happens, one day, she wakes up, she is in her thirties, she realizes that she is getting older, and the wall is coming.

She starts to get anxious that she may never find the one. She realizes that all of the younger marriage-minded women, who have prioritized having a family over a career, are scooping up the men she passed on.

She goes on dates and makes loud declarations to men, "I don't want to waste my time."

All the while not realizing that she is the one who wasted her time.

She wasted her time playing on online dating apps, dating men who were abusive, dating emotionally unavailable men, dating men who were half in, half out, and wasting her time chasing players, Chads, and the Tyrone's.

She is the one who wasted her time when she had the most value to marriage-minded men who wanted to settle down and have children.

I know right now this sounds very cold, and no doubt it must be very hard for most women to hear. But it's because I need to be brutally honest with you, and as I mentioned earlier, **I need to tell you like it is**, instead of sugar coating the truth about how some women can get in their own way of having what it is that they say they truly want out of life.

It is very difficult for a woman to squeeze school, career, traveling, giving herself time to experience life and to figure things out in such a small window.

No need to tell you that women are under tremendous pressure to try and figure everything out, and mother nature and men can be very cruel because they don't care about your biological clock.

You can make all your declarations while you are dating that you want, blame men, and society, refuse to do the deep inner personal growth work and refuse to heal and let go of your past wounds.

But know this, every year that you wait to **heal your wounds, change your dating habits, and your mindset** is another year that a fresh batch of twenty-somethings are coming out onto the dating scene.

As much as you hate it and don't want to admit it, they are your new competition for marriage-minded men.

Older women who want to have children and raise a family see the wall and, because of this, pressure men to move forward in their relationships much faster than he is comfortable with in order to meet their timeline.

Most men, given a choice, will take the younger version of you, someone he can take time to date without pressure and take the time to date for a few years before deciding to get married.

Younger women, who, because they are not facing the wall, may come off as much more agreeable than you and much easier to be with.

The fact is that marriage-minded women in their twenties and early thirties are grabbing what little marriage-minded and ready men there are.

And let's face it, in these modern times, not many men are marriage-minded. There is just too much for men to lose. 50% of his wealth, freedom, variety, and access to children if the relationship should fail, and yes, often, men are blamed for relationship failures.

The "system" and society are not kind to men in this regard, and men know it.

There is another problem women have to deal with, and that is **the risk of pregnancy**. This is something men don't have to worry about. They can make a mistake and just walk away. Women can't.

And trust me, I have worked with numerous single mothers. Life is hard raising children by yourself, and dating as a single mother is even harder.

Most men, regardless of age or access to resources, do not want to pay for another man's child or deal with the headache of that child one day saying, you are not my father, as well as always knowing that he will be forever a third wheel when it comes to decisions regarding the child, the child's discipline and the child's future, not to mention dealing with toxic exes.

So, why would he do it?

Again, the dilemma, what few marriage-minded men there are, have a very easy choice to make, date and marry a woman with children and all of the problems that will bring to him or date a woman with no children.

Because sooner or later, you will discover the age-old lesson that life experience and wisdom can only give you.

We all suffer from one of two pains in life. One is from **the pain of discipline,** or you can suffer the pain of regret.

When I speak to men and women, the one universal truth I hear is this. Women tend to regret the sex they had, especially the first time, and particularly if they got pregnant at a very young age.

Men tend to have the opposite attitude when it comes to sex. Men tend to regret the sex that they didn't have.

Men want to have sex with you for various reasons, either to play and have fun until he finally meets the one and is ready to get married, to further validate their ego, or to get married and create a family.

The choice is yours, which man you choose.

But if you get pregnant, know this, your future will be substantially much more difficult in almost every single way, but not for him.

And please don't misinterpret what I am saying. I am not saying that you cannot be happy and single for the rest of your life. But ask a single mother at 25, 35, or 45 whether she thinks it is a good choice to have children before finding a good husband to have children with.

Every single one of them, if they are being honest, will tell you that they wish they had married a good man before getting pregnant. They wish they had chosen a man who would have stuck around, a man who would have dedicated himself to his family, to be a good husband and a good father.

CHAPTER 4:
BIOLOGY – WHY MEN DO WHAT THEY DO...

INSIDE OUT DATING MAKEOVER

KEVIN BOYLE

There are so many things that I never understood about dating, about men, women, and relationships until I got much, much older. And I only wish that my father had taken the time to teach me what I'm about to share with you today when I was growing up.

So please make time to read this entire section. It is going to save you from a lot of confusion, heartache, and heartbreak, and it's going to go a very long way in helping you understand why things are the way that they are when it comes to understanding men dating, and having successful, loving, happy relationships.

And as I mentioned earlier, first off, I know there's probably a bunch of material in this book that is very politically incorrect, and you may disagree with.

Heck, you most likely already feel triggered by some of the things that I've already said, but you need to know this is coming from years and years of experience in helping women understand men in my own coaching business and working with all kinds of women at all ages to meet the man of their dreams.

And most importantly, **it comes from a father who loves his daughter very much.**

Have you ever heard the term, the war between the sexes? Sometimes it can feel that way.

Sometimes it feels like it's really hard to understand the opposite sex and why they do and say what they do.

It's because men and women generally approach dating and relationships very differently. And a lot of it comes down to biology, and unfortunately, because of political correctness, there is a lot of misinformation out there about the differences between men and women.

Pick up any dating or relationship book, and rarely do they talk about the true nature of men and the true nature of women, and I think this is where most women need the most help.

Not only understanding men but also understanding themselves.

Getting a man is easy for most women, but getting the right man? Almost impossible if you are doing what everyone else is doing.

Because men date for quantity and women date for quality.

So, let's address the elephant in the room.

SEX.

First, know that you cannot change biology. No amount of educating, socializing, shaming, nagging, or anything else will change men's biological behavior.

It is the way it is for a reason. It is this polarity that creates tension and sexual desire, and attraction between the sexes.

And as you probably know well by now, men are biologically wired to want to have sex.

And here is where it becomes an even larger problem for you. Because as you probably are well aware, **men fall in love with their eyes**. Your appearance is VERY important to men, and more often than not, this is what leads him to you. This is what attracts him to you.

But because men "fall in love with their eyes," **they may not even know if they like you.** They don't even know you well enough to see if you two are even compatible or not. All he knows is that you look good, and he WANTS you.

Often times you might NEED to SLOW him down and realize that **after he gets to know you, he might not actually like you.**

And here's the part that unfortunately many women do not quite fully understand.

While women control access to sex, men control access to relationships.

Just because you are having sex with a man does not mean that you are in a relationship with him. **Just because you had sex with a man doesn't mean you have him or that you got him.**

You might think you are, but most men use the **promise of a relationship** or the **promise of commitment** to get the cookie from women.

So, if you can understand this key critical concept in how men and women approach dating and relationships very differently, it will save you a lot of pain, heartache, and frustration.

Ever notice how many women complain about men not wanting to commit or having a hard time finding a good man who wants to have a relationship?

It's because most women do not understand this fundamental truth about dating and relationships and the differences between men and women.

Yes. Women get to choose who they are going to have sex with.

But the flip side of the coin is that men get to choose who they are going to have a long-term committed relationship with.

So many women make the mistake of thinking. I am pretty. I am in great shape, I have a great body, and I am everything men say they want. And he wants sex, he chased, he told me that I was the most amazing woman he had ever met.

So, you finally give in, and you give him the cookie.

But here's the problem.

When you use sex to get a man, there's a real danger that becomes the only value he sees in you. That's how you "got him," that's how you closed the deal in your mind, but he has a very different mind than you.

He wanted it, **and he said, and he did whatever he needed to say to get it.** So, if you like to travel, he likes to travel, if you like dogs, he likes dogs, and if you want a long-term committed relationship? Guess what! So does he!

Here's where you may have gone wrong. And who can blame you? Most likely, no one has ever taken the time to explain to you about what some men will do to get sex from a woman.

Some men will use the PROMISE of a relationship or the PROMISE of commitment to get sex from women, and promises get broken all of the time.

Most younger women make the mistake of giving in to sex way too early, thinking that that's what guys really want and thinking to themselves, I don't want to risk losing him, or I know it's going to make him happy, so I'll give it to him.

So yes, sex is what he wants, **but it's not** what gets him to commit.

So, women get frustrated because they don't get the guy, and they don't get the relationship that they want. So, they keep trying because they are doing what everyone else is telling them to do. And then, one day, they get mad, and over time, they become wounded, damaged, and disillusioned. And in doing so, they unwittingly make themselves less desirable because now they are jaded, now the body armor comes on, and their defenses go up.

Because what man wants to suffer because of your poor decisions, boundaries, and choices in men before him? What man wants to walk on eggshells and go through interrogations and declarations on first dates because you no longer trust men?

If you do not get this fundamental law about the basic differences between men and women, how they date, and how they approach relationships. You are going to experience a lot of pain in trying to find a good man to have a relationship with.

So yes, you do, you have control over the access to sex, but men control access to a relationship.

So, you have to be really honest with yourself.

If you are asking a man to wait. You need to ask yourself this one very critical question.

CHAPTER 5:
ARE YOU WORTH WAITING FOR?

INSIDE OUT DATING MAKEOVER

KEVIN BOYLE

Because just like you are evaluating him, he is evaluating you.

He is asking himself if you are worth waiting for. He's asking if you are wife material, if you are making good choices in men, or if you respect yourself. He is wondering if you have good boundaries and standards when it comes to men, if you have a good attitude towards men, and lastly, if you avoid playing games with men.

If you ask any man or woman at age 55, 65, or 75 and ask them if they wish to have spent more time in the office and more hours dedicated to their career. 99% of all men and women would say no. They would tell you they wish they had spent more time with their families and children.

Once you have a child, I can't tell you how much happiness and pure joy it adds to your life. My biggest source of happiness comes from time spent with my wife, daughter, and dog. A caveat, they also make me crazy, but I wouldn't have it any other way.

So why wouldn't you want a good man to share that with?

Yes, good men are boring. Nice guys are boring. I suppose I am boring. I don't go to Fiji every second weekend, I don't own a jet, I don't go to vineyards to sip wine every weekend, and I do not have the body of a professional athlete. But I do make an excellent husband, and I think I am a pretty good dad, just ask my daughter.

So, if you are not marriage-minded right now and do not ever envision having children either through adoption or natural childbirth, I would highly recommend you reconsider.

Children will fill your heart with joy and love; they are delightful, fun, full of life, and will change your life for the better.

So please know that I am not making the argument that women should not have any fun at all, not pursue higher education, not have a job or a career or not look after themselves and their independence as a capable and resourceful person.

I just want to take this opportunity to encourage you to take a step back, re-evaluate your life priorities, and look for the best way for you to find balance in your life to help you reach your goals, whatever they might be.

There is something else I want to take the time to talk to you about. I want to talk to you about a fairly taboo subject, one that most people would rather not discuss.

But we have gone this far, so why stop now?

Let's explore another aspect of biology and how this all plays out in dating and relationships.

Women, as you know, have estrogen as their primary hormone, and men have testosterone as their primary hormone. It's not to say that men don't have estrogen because they do and that women don't have testosterone because they do. But we are talking about ratios and amounts, and we are generalizing because the amounts found in men and women are generally quite different. Our hormones are a huge factor in what drives our biological needs and desires and how we see and experience the opposite sex in a relationship.

I can never give you the experience of being a man or a teenage boy with testosterone. But what I can do is try and explain it to you as best as I can so you can better understand how it influences men and how they behave on dates.

Have you ever been in a really fast car, or have you ever been on a roller coaster? They are so fast. Although it's very exciting, you can also feel like you are a little bit out of control.

This is how testosterone affects a man's body and his thinking.

Men have the most testosterone around the age of 18. Think about that. Men have the most testosterone around the age of 18, and they do not fully mature until age 30. Talk about mother nature being a little bit twisted and cruel!

It makes most males completely preoccupied with sex and girls. **At a time in their lives when they are least emotionally equipped to handle it.**

And because of this overwhelming desire and drive, most men will say or do almost anything to convince you to have sex with them.

You need to really understand this. It is the way men are built biologically. We as men cannot help the way God or mother nature made us. You cannot change us, and you cannot wish this away.

Three separate peer-reviewed studies were conducted by social psychologists from the University of Illinois, the University of Rochester, and the Interdisciplinary Center of Herzliya on why women date and end up marrying jerks.

Essentially it comes down to this because an attractive woman between the ages of 18 and 28 can pretty well have any man she wants. Men become "too" available. What happens when men make themselves too available and throw themselves at women? They become less desirable. I need you to really think about that for a minute.

When men make themselves too available to women, women lose interest and attraction towards them.

Why settle for the guy falling all over himself to be with me when I want, that guy over there, the guy who seemingly doesn't care or doesn't even know I exist.

The Chad's and the Tyrone's, the bad boys, the players, and the jerks.

The fact is women like a challenge just like men do. Women want what they can't have just like men, and trust me when I say this, you suffer because of it, and many women break themselves because of it, because if you want to have a family, if you want to have babies, women have a clock and men don't.

I have a story to share with you, and you are not going to believe this. You will think I am making this up, but this is completely 100% true.

When I was young and single and when I would go into bars. I have never in my entire life had a woman approach me, ever. Yet every single time I had a date with me, as soon as my date would go to the bathroom or walk up to the bar to get a drink, a woman would approach me and try to pick me up. It always blew my mind. There are tons of single guys sitting here in this bar wanting to meet a girl, but you approach me, the one guy who came in with his girlfriend.

So, here's the truth, women want to tame that tiger, the Chad's and the Tyrone's, because you love the challenge of getting a man you perceive as high value.

Just like men. You hate the game, but you love the highs and the lows of the chase, and just like men, you love the "win."

But here's the problem, what men consider a "win" and what you consider a "win" are completely different, and this is how women damage themselves, and this is why women should not be promiscuous like men, and **why you need to stop chasing men.**

But you don't.

Because for the same reason that you are indifferent to all of the "nice" guys or the "boring" guys who keep throwing themselves at you are the same reasons that the Chads and the Tyrone's are indifferent to you.

Generally, women date up. So, you have 60 to 80% of the women chasing 10 or 20% of the men.

Chad and Tyrone have women throwing themselves at them all the time.

Chad and Tyrone have many options, much more than the average guy, so why would they ever want to get married?

But let's say you do "get" him. Let's say you do get his attention, and he does ask you out.

You need to know this. **Most men do not want to be in the friend zone.**

So, over time Chad and Tyrone learn how to lie. In fact, they get really good at it.

CHAPTER 6:
BECAUSE MOST MEN LIVE FOR THE COOKIE.

INSIDE OUT DATING MAKEOVER

KEVIN BOYLE

Men plan how to get the cookie, and how to get it consumes his every thought. Men want to get you away from your friends and get you alone so they can get it. Some men will buy you alcohol in the hopes of getting you drunk and lowering your inhibitions so that you are more likely to give it to them.

Men will pretend they don't like you to get it.

Some men will love bomb you and tell you that they have never met anyone as beautiful, wonderful, and unique as you.

While other men will try to diminish you, the prettier you are, the more likely a man will try to pick out your flaws to make you feel self-conscious around him, to make you want to prove yourself worthy of him.

They will tell their friends that they think that you are ugly. Or, when they're around you, they will pick out something about you that you might be self-conscious about.

Some men will use any and all manipulations to try and get it. They will say, I just really like you, and I just want to feel your naked skin next to mine.

But you need to know this about men. Once they have obtained it, the hunt is over. The chase is over. The game is over.

Men like a challenge, and the best analogy I can use is that men will keep playing games that challenge them and that they enjoy.

So, if you are enjoyable to be around, playful, flirty, fun, **have high standards and strong boundaries,** and you are what he wants, a man will keep coming back to you.

But if the game is too easy, if the man finally beats the game and "wins" (gets the cookie), the game is done. The game gets put back on the shelf, and he simply moves on to a new, more challenging "game" to play.

I have talked to numerous men on this topic. Serious men looking for a relationship do not want you sleeping with them on the first date. They do not want you to have weak boundaries or low standards. They look forward to the challenge of having to win you over.

Because **no good man wants a win handed to him**. More often than not, men will tell me that it feels "too easy" and meaningless.

When I was thinking about this dynamic, I was trying to think of an analogy to help me better explain to you what I mean about this.

Imagine if you just started playing a brand-new video game. Imagine if when you entered the game, I gave you a max-level character with everything; all the outfits available, full gear, every place explored, etc. everything.

Would you really be excited about playing the game? Or would you feel cheated, as if **I took away the experience from you**? Yes, I gave you the win, "which is what you thought you wanted," but in doing so, I also made the game **way too easy for you.**

And there is a very good chance you might get bored and go find a different game to play.

Conversely, if you have been playing the game for a while, and you earn those things, over time you will start to become invested in your character. You will want to see your character grow, to overcome challenges, and to do well in the game.

Now let's put that in the context of dating and being intimate with men.

When you have sex with a man who is not committed to you. You just had sex with him. It doesn't mean you "got him." Sleeping with a man without a commitment from him gives you nothing.

A man will not commit himself to you just because you have slept with him.

So, in your mind, you convince yourself you can get 10's, but in reality, you never got a 10. You slept with a 10. But that 10 was never willing to commit to you because men **use the PROMISE of love and commitment to get sex.**

Men can afford to play, but if you spend too many of your best years chasing Chad's and Tyrone's, one day you might wake up, in your thirty's, single, and frustrated.

Frustrated because you believe men are using you for sex. But the reality is you passed by all the good ones who were willing to wait and work towards building a life and a future with you, and instead, you went for the player, and you got played.

You dropped your standards to get him. He doesn't have to always behave like a gentleman like those other guys, and here is the kicker. He doesn't have to wait for sex like those others guys. And then you get mad at him. You get angry at men because he does what bad boys do when women give themselves to them. He takes you for granted, and worst of all. He doesn't respect you.

Because now you are the one who is too "available."

So be prepared for the next day, when you are all flush, and you are thinking, oh my god, he's so great, maybe he's the one, he said he loved me and that we would be together forever, and he's so funny, he's so handsome, so caring, so charismatic, and he makes me oh so happy.

But now you have given him what he wanted, the game is over, the challenge is gone, and you are now at your most vulnerable.

This is not a flex on you. This is a flex on him. Because now that you have given yourself to him, he gives you breadcrumbs, just enough to make you think you might still have a chance. So, he tells you he is busy with work or has to study.

But who's fault is it really when you fall for the external just like men do?

When you over-invest in a man too soon because of his smooth, fast-talking, charming ways, because of his nice car, because he's so much fun, because of the way he makes you feel without knowing;

1. That he has proven himself to be a good man.
2. That he will treat you with respect.
3. That he is committed to you and you only.

Both men and women would be wise to **ALWAYS** keep the age-old advice of **"ACTIONS speak louder than words"** in mind when it comes to business, friendships, and more importantly with romantic partners!

And if you made the decision to give him sex without being in a committed, loving relationship with him where he is treating you with the utmost respect, there is a very good chance that you are going to be left.

Left wondering what the heck just happened?

Well, I'll tell you what the hell just happened. You got played.

And if you do this enough times, it will damage you. It will damage your attitude towards men, dating, and sex. You will stop trusting men, and you will stop trusting your choices in men.

So, before you have sex with a man, you have to be really clear with yourself. Is this really the man you want to share that part of yourself with? It's a big step.

Because when you fully understand what being the woman of his dreams means and what you need to do to be that woman, he will fully commit himself to winning you over.

He will do everything "right" because he does not want to ever take the risk of losing you. Because if he loses you, he's never going to be able to have the chance to be intimate with you.

And here's the ultimate truth that you need to hear; If he doesn't or won't, then **YOU ARE NOT the one.**

You need to stop pursuing men. Yes, go ahead and choose him, but he is the one who needs to commit. **Commit to the process** of getting to know you and winning you over. The reason why you want to leave the pursuit up to him is that it's the only reliable way for you to gauge interest and **how serious he is about you**. So, do not do his job for him!

When a man sees a future with you, he will leave no doubt in your mind by the amount of time he spends with you, how he treats you, and how hard he chases you.

The problem is that most women over-invest in a man before he invests in you because they make the very common mistake of falling in love with the external; he drives a nice car, he takes you to fancy restaurants, he has a great job or a great career, he's so charming, so funny, so worldly, just like men do when they fall in love with your appearance.

So, when the red flags come, **you don't leave when you should.** You start making excuses, lowering your standards, people-pleasing, and doing things that you might not otherwise do. Note; you can find some great examples of red flags on pages 118 and 122.

If any man ever draws a line in the sand and says to you that he lives by the three-date rule or that he will not have a relationship with you unless you have sex with him.

If this happens, you need to leave. You need to grab your stuff and go. It is a manipulation to get sex, and anything that comes out of his mouth will be a lie because you are not the one, you are a placeholder, and he sees you only as a plaything until he decides he is ready for marriage.

Sex should be a shared, mutual, joyful, connected experience of **two people on the same page**, not one person bending the will of another to their own.

CHAPTER 7:
BUT KEVIN, HE DOESN'T LIKE OPERA. THIS IS NEVER GOING TO WORK!

INSIDE OUT DATING MAKEOVER

KEVIN BOYLE

A common refrain I hear today from modern women is where are all of the good men? Let me assure you, there are tons of very good men.

How many times have you heard someone say, "If he had confidence, he would just be brave and come over and introduce himself? Wouldn't he?"

Actually, let's be completely honest. You are likely just as afraid of rejection as he is. So, you end up with the wrong guys approaching you, and you end up talking to men you are not even that interested in.

He's too short. He's too ugly.

You say you want a man to look deeper and appreciate you for more than just your body and your pretty face…

Men want the same thing.

They want a woman who sees past the superficial.

But you are not being 100% honest with yourself or with men. **You are probably being just as superficial in your dating preferences in men as they are with you.**

Most women will not even consider a man who is not taller than them.

Do you know how much of the male population is over 6'?

It's about 12%.

Do you know how many men make over 100k a year?

It's about 10%.

So, if we average that out, because not all men over 6' make over 100k a year, we are left with about 5% of men. Now, of that 5%, how many are married? I would say most.

Marriage-minded women grab marriage-minded men very fast because so few men are marriage-minded.

So, of the one man in one hundred available and who is in your "dating pool," how many are going to be physically attractive and handsome? How many are going to be funny? How many are outgoing? How many are going to have a great social circle of friends? How many are going to have a great relationship with their family? How many are going to own their own home? How many are going to be bold and adventurous? How many are going to be spiritual or of the same religion as you? How many are going to dress well? How many men are going to have habits or aspects about them that remind you of your ex? How many will enjoy the same hobbies and pastimes as you? How many are going to be the right star sign? How many are going to be high-status males? How many will be vegan, and lastly and most importantly, how many of those will be marriage-minded?

Did I forget anything?

Oh yeah, he must love cats because I see a lot of cats in your future…

When you are done with your list, there might be one man on the entire planet that is going to meet your dating criteria, and with your luck, he will probably be gay.

And because of this, you made it impossible.

Impossible for the one good man who would have made an excellent husband.

I had briefly mentioned this earlier in the book on page 17 of the first chapter, and in my opinion, **it is the single biggest mistake both men and women make** when it comes to finding a loving partner who wants to go the distance.

And it's this; **STOP focusing on what you want**. I guarantee you, you already know who he is. Trust me when I say this. You will know him when you see him.

Start focusing on who you are "being." **The very best version of yourself, the most powerful, confident, joyful, loving version of yourself.** The sooner you start focusing on this, the sooner he will appear.

That's it. That is **the secret** to attracting the most amazing man of your dreams.

CHAPTER 8:
UNDERSTANDING MEN. UNDERSTANDING THE HERO'S JOURNEY.

INSIDE OUT DATING MAKEOVER

KEVIN BOYLE

It's called The Hero's Journey because, fundamentally, men are looking for respect. Yes, your love is important, but underneath love, what is even more important to a man is your respect.

Not many women respect or want a broke, unemployed man as a marriage partner. So, men learn at an early age that they need to provide not only for themselves but for others.

They also learn that the world is a very dangerous place, so they need to protect what is important to them, and they also realize that to gain a woman's respect, keep her fully committed to the relationship, and be sexually attracted to her man, he must possess the attributes of a leader.

Provide, protect, and have the qualities of a leader.

This is when a man feels most fulfilled and most secure in a relationship with a woman when he feels respected.

And as part of a man's Journey, his Hero's Journey, a man must prove himself worthy not only to himself but worthy to his community and society, and in doing so, a by-product of that is status.

The Hero's Journey is a man's search for purpose and meaning in his life. Most men search for meaning and purpose outside of a relationship. Men go to the moon, climb mountains, and are driven to build great companies. This is a key difference in how men and women seek purpose and meaning in life.

A man's true purpose is not found in a relationship in the same way a woman's is, and this is not to say a man does not find purpose and meaning in a family or that a woman cannot find the cure for cancer and make that her life's goal.

But generally speaking.

Your drive as a woman is to be the hero to your children.

A man's drive is to be a hero to you, your family, and society.

Ladies, if your man has no job, no goals, no competence, no confidence, no vision, no passion. Deep down, you know what I am saying is 100% true, you are not going to feel a lot of respect towards him.

Therefore, the true driving force of most men, a core need for most men, is to DO something meaningful in their life and BE something meaningful to gain respect, admiration, and status.

His need to be a hero.

Your hero, if you let him.

Would it not be more empowering to help women better understand themselves and what attracts them to a man, better understand what drives men and what makes men want to commit to a relationship?

If a man doesn't make a decent income, he can't provide, if a man is not very masculine, he cannot protect, and if a man has zero status, a woman will not allow her man to assume a leadership role in the relationship.

Ultimately, if a woman does not admire her man and does not respect him, she may never truly love him, and that's why in my opinion, there are so many sexless marriages.

The studies are clear. Women initiate 70 to 90% of all divorces.

Meaning men are willing to commit and that once they commit, they commit for the long term. **Good men want to be your hero,** but more often than not, they feel beat down, they do not feel supported, and they do not feel encouraged.

It is women who are walking away from commitment, not men.

So, you might say, well, it's because there are so many bad men. Well, I know many very good men, very good men who are single and very good men who are married.

What the studies show is this, **women are very unhappy with the choices that they are making with men.**

So unhappy that they are willing to leave marriages and go out into a messy, chaotic, and unforgiving dating marketplace.

This is why in my opinion, it is so critically important for women to pick competent relationship partners from the very BEST version of themselves instead of from a place of loneliness, low-self esteem, damage, neediness, or a need for validation.

Because quite simply, if you don't, it can be very disastrous for you and your future, especially if you decide to have children with this man.

Maybe if you were to be 100% honest with yourself and hold yourself accountable as much as you want to hold men accountable, you would realize that, unfortunately, far too many **women create their own drama** by continuing to make poor choices in men.

Because that's what I was doing, making poor choices in women.

And over time, you get angry, you get frustrated. You start to lose hope that you will ever find a good man (even though you friend zone the good ones because they're too nice or too boring).

In time, you proudly proclaim to your friends and to men who you are dating, "I am strong and independent, and I don't need a man!"

I get it, I understand, you may have never known the love of a good man, a man who truly loves and respects you, so you try to protect yourself with your words, your attitude, and your armor.

But here's the problem, yes, I agree 100%, you do not "need" a man.

But here's the kicker. Yes, you may not need a man, **but your children do.**

Despite what other women might tell you, your children need a good father.

Having a father with a strong masculine presence in their lives means that children have higher outcomes in life, relationships, self-esteem, development, and achievement.

Boys and girls need fathers.

Children who grow up with involved fathers are more likely to do much better in school, 80% less likely to get in trouble with the law, twice as likely to go to college and find stable employment after school, 75% less likely to get pregnant in their teens, and most importantly, **have much less difficulty in forming loving, committed, long-lasting, successful relationships.**

Your children need a good man, a good father, and a good role model, and yes, **they need to see what a good husband looks like through your choices in men.**

You need to model that for your child, and you need to model that for future generations.

And yes, I will agree it is a huge burden for women, but Gandhi said it best when he said, "be the change you wish to see in the world."

As I had mentioned earlier in the book, it is so easy to point at the opposite sex and say that they are the ones that are the problem. That men need to grow up, that men need to heal, and that most men will never do the work.

The reality is, so do women.

Women need to realize that, yes, how you are on the outside will attract a man, but how you are on the inside is what keeps him and gets him to commit.

What I have found after working with hundreds of women is that women need to heal, too.

Women need to stop chasing love, that is not chasing them.

Women need to stop chasing love, that is not available to them.

Women need to stop chasing love, that is damaged.

Women need to stop chasing love, that is hurting them.

Women need to stop making babies with men who have no interest in becoming good fathers.

The general rule of thumb is pretty straightforward and pretty simple, if you have not found yourself a good husband, who you know is competent in life, don't make a baby.

The reality is that if a man wants to have sex (and he does), men are taught by women what works.

And what works is being the bad boy. While men look for danger in their hobbies and activities, women will often look for danger in the men they date, and the men they fall in love with.

When dating, you tell men that you don't have time for games. Yet a common mistake made by many women is that they always seem to "fall" for the bad guys because the good guys, those who don't play games, are too "boring."

But here is the painful part, the wall is undefeated, **and the players, the Chads, and the Tyrone's remain uncommitted.**

Ultimately, if we as a society want men to be better, we need to do our part.

We need to take more responsibility for our choices in men.

CHAPTER 9:
IT'S TIME TO CHANGE THE RULES OF DATING, WHERE YOU CHOOSE, AND HE COMMITS!

INSIDE OUT DATING MAKEOVER

KEVIN BOYLE

From now on, either you give him permission to approach you, or you approach him.

This is your new BOUNDARY and your new STANDARD in dating.

Listen, I get it. We all have a fundamental need to feel like we have been chosen. But be 100% honest with me, how is it working out so far? Not very well, is it?

And at what price? In order to feel validated, in other words, to say or feel like "someone chose me," we have to give up OUR power.

Most women let men choose because that's how it's "always" been done and because no one likes to risk feeling or being rejected, and lastly, it helps feed our need for validation.

A woman wants to be able to say, yes, a man chose me, that not only a man chose me, but **the best man chose me**, that I am worthy, that I am the prettiest girl in the room, that yes, I am desirable.

And it is the biggest mistake you will ever make in dating and the biggest reason you are still single. And more importantly, if you present yourself as a "trophy," most men will treat you like a trophy.

Men will chase you for the win, for ego gratification. And what do men do with a trophy after winning? Sooner or later, they put it back up on the shelf and go find a new game to play.

Have you ever heard the stories about women losing husbands to the new receptionist at work? This is why.

And this is why you need to take CONTROL of your dating and your love life.

Why not be proactive in who you choose to meet 100% of the time?

Where you choose, he commits.

You pick the man you want; you open the door, you choose who approaches you, you approach men who you are interested in, you choose who to invest your time in, and you choose who to be friends with.

The old patriarchal way of dating and mate selection that goes back hundreds and hundreds of years where you are an "object of men's desires" waiting to be chosen is an old, outdated dating model that needs to go.

No longer do you need to sit on the sidelines of your life, hands politely folded on your lap, waiting for Mr. Right.

It's time to take control, be BOLD and start living your life as the most POWERFUL, confident, joyful, loving version of yourself!

So, you might be asking yourself, Kevin, this doesn't seem very feminine. In fact, isn't it the man's job to approach, chase, and pursue?

Yes, it is. Nothing has changed. In fact, way back in the day, women dropped their handkerchiefs to show interest in a man and let him know they wanted him to approach and introduce himself.

But now, you are simply being much more proactive in how you choose a man and in how you are OPENING the door to let him know that you are interested, available, and approachable.

The rest is still up to him.

The courting, the pursuing, and the chasing are still up to him.

And to be clear, opening the door is not the same as chasing.

It's time to finally STOP letting your fear, insecurities, and society's outdated and antiquated dating rules make your life decisions for you.

Ultimately what happens in your life is that when you let your fears run the bus, when you let fear control you, you will start basing all of your decisions on whether you are willing to feel uncomfortable or not, and this is how we "self-sabotage" this is how we abandon ourselves, our futures, and our dreams.

Just ask my daughter. Since she was six years old, I have always told her to be brave, bold, kind to others, and show up for herself.

And when you do this, when you are the brightest light in the room because you are showing up for yourself. You will "own the room," and you will be the only woman he will ever want in his life.

Because as much as you love confidence in a man, men love confidence in a woman.

Why is it so important for you to take control and for you to do the choosing?

An analogy I like to use for better understanding men and their dating mindset is to think of it as climbing a mountain. Let's use climbing Mount Everest as an example.

Men are always looking to conquer, and for the greatest possibility of a "win," this is a man's way of filling his validation needs. Because yes, men do like a challenge, but they like winning even more.

If you make the possibility of even thinking about climbing Mount Everest impossible. (Read, if you are difficult, if you are demanding, if you act entitled, or if you act like a snob or aloof).

No good man wants to ever pursue or approach a woman who does not reciprocate interest.

But not the bad guys and the wannabe players. They see your coldness and your unapproachability **as a CHALLENGE to be overcome.**

So inadvertently, the good guys will not approach. Because your demeanor is saying no, your attitude is saying no, and your body language is saying no.

What to do when a man you don't know asks you for your number, Snapchat, or Instagram.

You say; "I am very flattered, thank you. But I am not interested."

Woah, back up the bus, Kevin! I want to meet men, not tell them I am not interested! What kind of dating coach are you anyway? Pffft!

It's because you need to know this about men. TEN times out of ten when a man approaches you without a green light from you, meaning you did not give him permission to approach through a smile, your eyes, or a hello. He is most likely a player.

Men date for quantity, and women date for quality.

It's nothing more than a game to him. It's almost like playing a video game to him. "Oh, she looks hot. I wonder if I can get her number or her Snapchat?"

He is thirsty, **hoping you are thirsty.**

Any man who can cold approach you, has probably done this multiple times before, perhaps hundreds and hundreds of times to improve his confidence, approach, and delivery, perfect his game, and ultimately for bragging rights with his friends.

They're called "pick-up artists," so when he approaches you, you must also realize that he might be married, dating someone else, or he is a wannabe player.

From now on, either you give him permission to approach, or you approach him.

NO MORE THIRSTY MEN! No more cold approaches. No more thirsty boys or men sliding into your dm's looking for thirsty girls. No more thirsty men at bars.

Save yourself from a ton of grief, heartache, and pain.

Your response to cold approaches is always the same; "I am very flattered, thank you. But I am not interested."

So, how do you know a guy is genuine in his approach to you?

He waits for your permission. He waits for a green light. He waits for a signal from you that it is ok to approach.

Because in the age of the "me too" movement, it's just too risky to approach you without permission. What man wants to be seen as a predator or as "creepy"?

Most good men are not going to pursue a woman who does not reciprocate interest.

CHAPTER 10:
SELF-CHECKUP, ARE YOU READY TO DATE?

INSIDE OUT DATING MAKEOVER

KEVIN BOYLE

1. I know how to say no, and maintain my boundaries when needed.
2. I spend time with people who support, energize, and inspire me.
3. I have two or more close friends in my life.
4. I have a very healthy attitude towards men, dating, and relationships.
5. I am living a life of abundance. I have a great hobby or activity to look forward to in my life other than men, a relationship, or dating.
6. Now, imagine you are 16. What advice would you give yourself?
7. If you were going to sabotage yourself when it comes to men, dating, and a relationship, how would you do it?
8. What do you do to avoid feeling?
9. I have healed and let go of my wounds from the past. I am mature. I am powerful, confident, loving, secure, and full of life!
10. I know I am not being selfish when I put my own needs first. That is something that others have to earn from me over time by showing me that they have my best interests at heart and that they truly care about me.

CHAPTER 11:
ARE YOU THE MOST AMAZING WOMAN OF HIS DREAMS?

INSIDE OUT DATING MAKEOVER

KEVIN BOYLE

Once you have done your check-up and you feel like you are ready to date, and now knowing the nature of men, the question now becomes, how do you make it so you are the only mountain he wants to climb?

I am going to share something else about men that no one has ever told you, something about men that you need to know.

If you wait to have sex with a man, know that the most powerful drug known to a man is a woman that he finds beautiful, that he has not been intimate with yet.

You will always be on his mind.

He will always be trying to win you over and prove himself worthy of you, and a by-product of this, despite his protests to the contrary, is that you will earn his respect.

Go check out all of these men's channels on YouTube, Podcasts, and LISTEN very carefully. Men all say the same thing to other men. Do not marry a promiscuous woman!

Talk about mixed and confusing messages for women.

But it's always been the same since the dawn of time. Men want to have sex with you, but men do not want to marry a girl who is promiscuous.

It is the duality of men. They want to sleep with you, but they do not want it to be easy because a high-value woman has "standards" in his eyes. **He wants to do what very few other men have been able to do.** Which is win you over!

So, here's the deal. If you are the one, if you are fit and take care of your body, if you are playful, feminine, confident in who you are, easy to be with and fun, and you genuinely like men, **he will generally wait until you are ready.**

But this is also something you need to know about men and sex.

ALL men want sex. The "good" ones, the "nice" ones, and the "bad" ones. Just because a man wants to have sex with you doesn't mean he is "bad," has a hidden agenda, or is untrustworthy.

But here's the difference between a "good" man and a man who just wants to have sex with you.

The "good" ones, the ones who see a future with you. **Are willing to wait**, but only if you are worth waiting for.

So that becomes the million-dollar question, are you worth waiting for?

Because here's the truth, a good woman is a prize, and so is a good man.

If you are serious about "winning," have you ever considered being what he wants? Because if you haven't or won't, **he will most likely find someone else who will.**

Here's the ugly truth, here's where you need to drop your ego.

Have you ever considered that how you are "showing up" for men might not be working?

And maybe this is why.

CHAPTER 12:
WHY DOES MY SIX-YEAR-OLD SELF HAVE TO RUIN EVERYTHING?

INSIDE OUT DATING MAKEOVER

KEVIN BOYLE

I know that there are some bad men out there. Some men who use and some men who abuse women. Some men who are damaged and unable to commit because of their own wounds. That's why in my opinion, it is so critically important for most women to work on and through any issues they might have that are affecting their self-esteem, their confidence, and their ability to set healthy boundaries in their relationships.

I know I was damaged in some way from my upbringing. It took me a long time to figure out how to heal my wounds and how to heal and let go of my unhealthy relationship patterns and behaviors.

For the next section, I want to take a moment and quote from my first book, "From Breakup to THRIVING in 30 Days or Less," to help you better understand how and why our childhood self tends to wreck havoc in the majority of our relationships and why we have in my opinion such a high divorce rate in our society.

New studies show that there are certain memories, events, and experiences that stay with us from childhood that deeply affect how we see ourselves throughout our lives. They are called implicit memories, and they become the lens through which we see and experience our world and our relationships.

What we are told, what our parents model for us for the first 6 yrs. of our lives, shape how we live our entire lives. If your parents are emotionally unavailable, overly critical, or abusive. We will carry this relationship dynamic we had with our parents into every relationship and out on every single date we go on.

These beliefs stay with us our entire adult lives, manifesting themselves in our relationships and ultimately in who we attract and who we think we are worthy of. If these beliefs are "negative," there is a very good chance that they will manifest themselves in our relationships, causing chaos, pain, and suffering for ourselves and our relationship partners.

Our parents influence us in so many different ways. What our parents tell, teach and model for us, **we become and what they withhold from us, what they do not give us. We will look for in others.**

My father never gave me the validation I so desperately wanted and needed as a child. It created an emptiness deep inside of me that I could never fill. I always felt like I was searching. Because who could ever be enough, who could EVER **fill that void** that was deep inside of me?

If we take an objective look around, there are happily married people out there who have found their one special person. And it's no fun and certainly humbling when you come to realize that maybe the one constant in all of this frustration of trying to find "the one" is… you!

I had always known that, at some level, I had carried around with me this belief from childhood that I was not good enough, and as I sit back and reflect on it now, I realize that most of the time, I never had the words for it. I could just feel it.

Whenever I dated someone who I perceived as being more than me, "more together than me," more confident and competent than me, I could feel a subtle shift deep down inside; where I felt not good enough, and as I felt myself shift, I would start to feel very insecure and very needy. Like I needed to prove myself.

How many times have you resisted acknowledging that you are with the wrong person, that you are not being treated properly, that you are attracted to the wrong types of men, that you have stayed too long, or that the wrong types of men always seem to be attracted to you or maybe just maybe because of your painful past you are resisting true intimacy and real vulnerability with your partners.

Your resistance to acknowledging what is and what you need to do about it allows it to persist in your life and follow you from relationship to relationship.

Yes, some people hurt me deeply in relationships, but in hindsight, I also know I missed or chose to ignore the red flags.

I chose to over-invest myself in people who were never there for me but who were what I thought I "wanted." I chose to be in relationships that were not healthy for me because I didn't want to be lonely anymore, but more importantly, I had this script running deep within my subconscious mind that because I was so screwed up, because my life was so screwed up. **I needed someone "more" than me,** better looking, smarter, more responsible, and more competent, **to help save me from myself.**

I showed up for dates hurt and wounded from my past relationships, and I also showed up on dates insecure in the person that I was. I didn't trust people, and ultimately, I would self-sabotage and push the good ones away because of that lack of trust.

More often than not, if we are not happy with the results we are seeing in our lives, **we need to turn the spotlight back on ourselves.**

If I am being completely honest with you. I did it all. People hurt me, and I know I hurt others, and maybe just maybe if you can be really honest with yourself. You might be able to see a bit of yourself in my story.

But more importantly, more importantly than all of my dysfunctional behaviors and my dis-empowering limiting beliefs.

I showed up on dates and in relationships, hurt, wounded, and looking for validation.

Many of us say we are looking for a long-term relationship, that we are looking to get married, but in reality, we are unintentionally and unwittingly deceiving ourselves.

What most of us are really looking for is validation from and through our romantic partners.

Validation that we are enough.

And some of us never get enough, no matter how many people we date, no matter how many likes or comments we get on social media, or no matter how many people we sleep with.

The truth is, no one can ever fill that hole that is deep inside of us.

And that's when it clicked for me. That's when I made the shift.

I came to the realization that If I didn't change the way I felt about my life, about myself. Nothing was ever going to change for me when it came to my dating and romantic life.

And when you finally get it, when you too make that shift in perspective, that yes, maybe it is me, maybe I need to go inside and see what's going on and make some fundamental changes in how my mindset, my attitude, and most importantly my beliefs and how they are getting in my way of having the kinds of relationships that I say I want.

That's when your shift can happen, and your journey can finally begin.

As mentioned earlier in the book, it was very easy for me to look at the opposite sex and make blanket statements about how they were the cause of all of my pain and frustration when it comes to dating and relationships.

But this book is for you, about YOU **making a POWERFUL inside-out, life-changing transformation**. Because we cannot change something if we are unwilling to take responsibility for our part in how we show up in our dating and in our relationships.

A very common mistake most of us make when thinking about our next relationship is thinking about **who we want him to be** rather than **who we want to be.**

Because it's not just about what he did "wrong," it's about taking a closer look at what you may have done wrong.

It's about us taking responsibility in how we choose to show up in our relationships and what we can learn about ourselves. By taking an honest, objective look within.

By finally deciding to heal and let go of our disempowering limiting beliefs, unhealthy relationship patterns, behaviors, fears, and insecurities. I promise you that when you decide to take that journey, it will change how you experience others in relationships and how they experience you.

You will feel lighter, many of my clients feel like a huge burden has been lifted off of their shoulders. The best way I can describe it is to imagine you are outside on a warm sunny day, walking in a meadow on the side of a mountain, feeling the sun warm your face and skin—your mind is clear, feeling like anything is possible.

Here are some of the most common problems I find when working with single successful women wanting to meet high-quality men who are looking for long-term committed relationships;

- You were damaged in some way in your childhood. Perhaps you had an abusive father, an overbearing mother, or an overly critical parent. It doesn't matter because the effect on you is the same. Because you are wounded and never went to get help and to heal your wounds, you show up as either anxious or avoidant. Therefore, you attract or are attracted to men who are mirrors of you, which leads to a lot of "messiness," chaos, and disappointments in men and your relationships.

- You are so focused on finding the right person that you have completely forgotten about what it takes to become and to **BE the RIGHT person.**

- Deep down, if you are being really honest with yourself, you don't trust men, so men who do date you have to walk on eggshells because you are just waiting for them to make a mistake. And most men, even the good ones, make a lot of mistakes.

- You think that all men are dogs, all men are jerks, players, etc. Actually, no, just the ones you stay with. Most women, when they find out a guy is a jerk, a player, emotionally unavailable, or abusive, leave. But not you. You stay, and it damages you.

- You think that all men "just" want sex, so you play it too safe, trying to protect yourself, but during the date, you come across as cold, not very playful, not very much fun, too nice, and way too boring.

- That maybe, just maybe, you have been hurt or wounded one too many times, so you unwittingly bring this damaged person that is deep inside of you on to every date with you, into every relationship you ever have, and that if you are being 100% honest with yourself, you have grown scared, untrusting and aloof.

- And as soon as someone **touches on your wounds,** you get even messier, or more often than not, you pull back, or you push away because you are consumed with the thought that you might get hurt again.

- That all men are jerks or bad boys, but then you think, maybe I am not good enough. Besides, have you seen my hip dips, my cellulite, that big red pimple on my nose, or my big arms? How could anyone like or love me?

- You are so busy with your career that you only have time for dating apps.

- You either stopped caring about your appearance, or you never cared.

- You are so guarded or picky that you don't give any man permission to approach. So, the men who do have the courage and the "game" to approach you are exactly the kind of men you say you don't want.

- You mistakenly think that being a challenge to men is being difficult, demanding, and unapproachable.

- Just like you probably don't enjoy a man who shows up on a date with too much feminine energy, most men feel the same way about a woman who shows up on dates "stuck" in her masculine energy.
- That picking, attracting, and staying with partners poorly, seems to be a pattern in your life, so now you think all men are evil or that all men are users, abusers, players, or cheaters.

These are just some of the reasons you might be getting in your own way of meeting the most amazing man of your dreams to share your life with.

Have you ever considered that maybe, just maybe, you need to **REINVENT yourself** by having a complete inside-out, life-changing dating makeover and transformation?

And how do I know this works?

Because I see it in my twelve-year-old daughter. At a time when pretty well every single girl and boy in my daughter's class at school is either boy or girl crazy. My daughter has no interest in boys or girls. She is focused on friends, school, her hobbies, and enjoying her life.

My wife and I spend at least an hour a day with our daughter. I pride myself on having a very good, supportive, and loving relationship with my daughter, **where she knows she "is enough" just the way she is** and that she can talk to me about anything, and that I will not judge her.

I've tried my best to let her know that I want her to show up, take up space, that she can be anything that she sets her mind to be, and not worry about what others say or think about her.

And I knew I had to take care of my own demons first before I could ever model for her what a powerful, confident, joyful, loving person looks like.

So, I did.

One of my clients said it best when she said this to me. "Kevin, I wish I had known about this work twenty years ago. It would have saved me from so much pain, heartache, and regret!"

CHAPTER 13:
THE SEVEN STEPS TO YOUR INSIDE OUT DATING MAKEOVER.

Attracting: STOP focusing on what you want in a man. You will know him when you see him. **Start focusing on being the "right" person.** The sooner you start focusing on this, the sooner he will appear.

That's it, that is **the secret.**

Meeting: It's time for you to stop sitting on the sidelines of life with your hands politely folded on your lap, waiting for the one, and it's time for you to do the choosing.

"Being the right person." The Five Steps to Commitment.

Keeping your man happy and committed to you and your relationship is remarkably easy when you follow these five steps.

1. Activate your SUPERPOWER; Femininity.
2. Do you know how to be a challenge and how to be fun and flirty at the same time?
3. Do you have vulnerable, heartfelt conversations with your man?
4. Never stop being his girlfriend.
5. Life only gives you more of who you are being. Dating with an abundance mindset.

Attracting: Does your smile radiate from the inside out when you enter a room? Have you done the "work"? Are you your most irresistible, powerful, confident self?

Because this is the mistake that most women make when dating, I am the "prize," so I only need to focus on what I am looking for in a man, so much so that you completely forget what it takes to be the right woman.

As soon as I saw my wife's smile and eyes, I was done. It only took seconds. I knew from that moment that Maggie was the girl for me, and you really need to pay attention right now to what I am about to say;

At that moment, **I made the decision, the decision to do everything right** because I did not want to ever risk losing her.

How did I know?

Because her eyes and her smile told me everything I needed to know about her. Her eyes and her smile told me that she was happy, that she was approachable, and that she was warm, inviting, playful and feminine.

So, here's my question. What are your eyes, your smile (or lack thereof), and your body language telling men about how open and approachable you are?

Because, if you find yourself saying or thinking that all men are jerks, that all men are only interested in only one thing, that all men are users, that there are no good men left, or that I am not good enough, or that you don't trust men.

That becomes your energy and your attitude towards men. Your "energy" will introduce you before you even speak.

Because when you are wounded, you are not fully available. You are only available to offer small, measured-out pieces of yourself to a man, and in doing so, you hurt your chances of ever having a healthy, fulfilling relationship with men.

And yes, I get it. Men are damaging you. But when you are dating wounded or damaged, you are part of the cycle, and you need to get out of it.

I see it all the time, men and women **who no longer like or trust** the opposite sex, **and they still keep dating** because they feel lonely, empty, or bored.

But know this; you are part of the problem because broken people break people.

I know because I was one of those people. I needed someone to love me because **I didn't FULLY love myself**, and I hurt a lot of people along the way trying to get it.

So, don't be that person, and then I need you to know this.

I know you are hurt. I know you are wounded, but when you say those things, you are diminishing and shaming ALL men because of either your poor choices in men, having little to no boundaries with men, or dropping your standards for guys who you are attracted to.

You need to know that not all men are bad.

If you find yourself saying these things, **it's because of YOUR experiences with men.**

No healthy guy who is ready and wants to give you all the things you say you want wants to hear about all of the horrible men you dated before him.

Because that's what it becomes. You stop trusting men because you haven't done the work to clear out the hurt from your past relationships or maybe as far back as when you were a little girl. You carry it forward from relationship to relationship, from guy to guy, and if and when you do meet a good guy, a healthy guy, he runs for the hills.

Because when you say all men just want is sex, all men are jerks, or my last boyfriend was a "fill in the blank, "… you dimmish men.

You are shaming men for how they are biologically hard-wired. Would you seriously want to be on a date with a man who is complaining about hypergamy or that most women will not date him because he is too short?

Most men do not want to be with a woman who is shaming or diminishing men because of her bad experiences with them, just like you do not want to be with a man who diminishes or shames women because of his bad experiences with women.

The one thing I remember about Maggie is that on our first date, she never mentioned sex once, she never talked about how all men are jerks, she never talked about her exes or any of that, and she won me completely over.

I remember how refreshing it was to be on a date with a woman who did not complain about her ex or men, and I also remember how she was so playful, fun, flirty, feminine, and easy to be with.

Women say men are afraid of a strong independent woman. It's not that, if you know Maggie, you know that she is very strong and independent. Most men are not sexually attracted to women who display masculine energy or traits.

Just like most women are generally not attracted to feminine men.

Therefore, if men are looking for a partner who is feminine, what are most women generally looking for? Well, it turns out most women look for the opposite. Women generally look for men with a strong masculine "frame." I think we can all understand the masculine part. But Kevin, what do you mean by frame?

The frame is about my boundaries as a man. What I am willing to tolerate and what I am not.

Women need to have strong boundaries when they date men. **Men need to have strong boundaries when it comes to life**.

Men learn if we are too nice, if we take on the characteristics of the feminine. We don't get the girls, and if you don't get the girls, you don't get the cookie.

The second reason is that people start to treat men without a strong masculine frame, like a doormat.

It's because men learn that in our culture and our society, when men are too soft and lack a masculine frame, they tend to be exploited by their bosses, wives, and girlfriends.

This means he's going to make less money at work, and he is going to be miserable at home. He's not going to move up the corporate ladder, he's not going to be able to provide for his family, and sooner or later, his wife or girlfriend is going to lose a ton of respect for him and most likely lose sexual interest in him as well.

Therefore, men are taught by strong masculine fathers to have and maintain a strong masculine frame in all aspects of their life.

Because a man needs to earn the respect you want to give him and the respect that he needs to find for himself so he can fully become a man that can navigate and handle life's dangerous and chaotic waters.

If your man does not have a strong masculine frame, there will be a part of you that will start to lose respect for him, maybe even resent him. I see it all of the time, strong women caught up in the women's movement go for feminine men who will bend to their will, and then they regret it later.

So, here's the problem women face. Women need to find a man who is not only going to be a good provider, but you need to pick a man with a strong masculine frame because he is going to be the role model for their children and future generations.

But not so masculine that he is abusive or toxic.

It's all about respect, a man can be somewhat disagreeable, but does he respect you? Can he be kind and thoughtful at the same time as he is disagreeable?

Because to me, having a strong masculine frame is all about having a backbone, not about being a jerk.

So here is my promise to you when you do this deep inner healing work. When you heal the wounds of your past, when you heal and let go of your disempowering limiting beliefs, unhealthy relationship patterns, your fears, and insecurities, and when you stop looking for validation through men.

You will show up differently in your life and in your relationships, and you will show up differently for men.

And when you do this, when you finally remove your triggers, your defenses, your weapons, and your armor. You will start to evolve into being what I call the "highest version of yourself."

A person who radiates confidence, power, joy, and love, by who they are being.

A person who is smiling from the inside out becomes a man or a woman who is absolutely irresistible!

And when you show up differently for men, their experience of you changes.

And when their experience of you changes, your experience of them changes.

And it's at that moment where I made the decision, the decision that I was going to do everything right because I did not ever want to take the risk of losing her.

CHAPTER 14:
MEETING; WHERE ARE ALL THE GOOD MEN?

INSIDE OUT DATING MAKEOVER

KEVIN BOYLE

It's time for you to stop sitting on the sidelines of life with your hands politely folded on your lap, waiting for the one, and it's time for you to choose.

The question is, how to ensure that the right man approaches you. Because they are left up to their own devices, if you sit and wait for men to approach you, nine times out of ten, it will be the wrong one.

Because no need to tell you as a modern society we have a huge problem, as I alluded to earlier in the first chapter of this book. Dating and relationships today are chaotic and very messy. In response, a lot of men and women have simply given up and "checked out", and who can blame them.

Social media, where most girls are under constant pressure to look a certain way, even though we know a lot of those pictures have been photoshopped, creating impossible standards for women to live up to.

Boys who are easily influenced through underground communities, porn sites, and hip-hop songs to be more gangster, or by diminishing and degrading women.

That's why I highly recommend later on in this Chapter for women who want to meet men for committed long-term relationships to **stay away from** social media, dating apps, meeting men in bars, and allowing men to cold approach **as a way of meeting men.**

We need to empower our daughters and women of all ages.

Where women take control of where and how they meet men.

Where women do the choosing, not men.

Where women take the time to create genuine friendships with men.

Because **men are less likely to abuse, disrespect, or diminish a woman who he considers a friend.**

You choose where you are going to meet him, you choose when you are going to meet him, you choose why you are going to meet him, and then, and only then, if you are truly being what he wants, he will commit himself fully, because you are exactly what he is looking for.

You choose, he commits.

Maybe it's just in my experience. But over time I have learned that the best things in life are rarely easy. The best things in life **are often very hard to attain.**

So, why are you trying to make it so easy?

Why are you on dating apps?

Why are you meeting men on social media?

Why are you meeting men in bars?

Why are you accepting the absolute minimum effort from men and not insisting that they take the time and make an effort to date and court you?

The reality is most of the men you are meeting are probably not ready for a serious relationship. That is why they are on dating apps and social media.

You have to ask yourself, do you want a mature, responsible man who is ready for a serious relationship, or someone who is still trying to figure out his life and his finances?

So, when you ask where all of the good men are, the answer is easy.

Good men are at school upgrading their skills and their knowledge so they can get a better job or a good career.

Good men contribute to society by building things and volunteering their time at community-minded organizations.

Good men are out and about and engaging in their hobbies and interests.

Good men are working and busy building great companies.

Good men are friends of your friends. The more and the better-quality friends you have, the more chances you will have of meeting a good high-quality man.

If you are serious about meeting a high-quality man. You need to get social and go old school. It is the best way to meet people, it is the best way to observe people over time, and it is the best way to truly get to know someone.

When?

Then the question becomes, when is the best time to meet a man?

The best time to meet a man is when you have had a chance to see him over and over again, interacting in his environment, in your community with him, and with your peers.

How does he treat others? How does he treat co-workers? Is he a leader when he is in a group? How does he contribute? Is he fun? Is he stoic? Is he masculine? Is he competent? Does he have a temper? Is he controlling?

Your attraction to him over time will be based on true compatibility and truly seeing him for who he is, rather than blind sexual chemistry and hormones.

Why?

Because over time, he has proven to you that he is worth investing your time into.

Because you say you want men to be friends first, this is how you do it.

Because when you do it this way, there is no pressure on either of you to "perform," to be a certain way, to impress, or based on the pleasing of others.

Because when you do finally decide to give yourself to him, you will know that he is already committed to you and that hopefully over time he has proved to you that he is a good man.

Because whether you are an introvert, an extrovert, or just plain shy, this method of meeting men works for everyone!

And lastly and most importantly, if you take anything away from this section of the book, it is this.

If a man is spending time with you, getting to know you, and NOT making moves on you, it doesn't mean that he doesn't like you. In fact, it means he does like you, and the reason he is not making a move is that he is a good guy and he respects what you have, which is a friendship!

And women are always saying that they want men to be their "best friend."

Well, guess what? This is the way you do it.

This is absolutely the best way, in my opinion, for a woman to meet a man. I will cover more ways as we get further into the book. But if you are truly serious about finding and meeting a good man, this is the way to do it.

Get active. **Get out of the house** and get off of dating and social media apps.

Put more time into your social calendar to do the things that you enjoy doing to help give you more opportunities to meet men in person.

See the last chapter (starting from page 193) for different suggestions on where you can meet high-quality men.

The "what" and the "how" to meet good men.

Men want what they can't have. Men love a challenge, they love to chase, and they love to hunt.

But most importantly, men obsess over what they don't have.

So, give him what he wants; the gift of not knowing and the gift of not having.

During this time, YOU MUST commit to the process of getting to know him as a person and a friend.

Know that if you commit to the process of being truly feminine around him, if you are soft, if you are sweet, if you are happy to see him, if you take an active interest in who he is and what he is doing, you will become absolutely irresistible to him, **and he will commit himself fully to trying to figure out how to win you over.**

You are not some girl he met on a dating app. You are not some girl he met at a party, or in a bar, or some girl he tried to pick up at Starbucks.

You are now someone special, you are now a friend, you are now someone he cares about.

Your intention is to be open, inviting, and warm and to create opportunities for conversations. Conversations that allow you to get to know him better over time.

Not clingy, not needy, not pushy, no agenda.

Ask him for his help with something.

Ask him for his opinion on something.

You must read him properly. How does he react? Is he happy to help you or indifferent?

Find an excuse to lightly touch him in a very seemingly innocent way, and see his reaction. Does he turn to you and smile, or does he seem annoyed and pull away?

In time, when you feel like you have really gotten to know him and he has had a chance to get to know you, trust me if you have done this right, he will want you more than he has ever wanted any other woman.

Then one day, while you are chatting. Give him the green light and casually mention it to him.

You: "It's been such a long time since I've been… What about you?"

And then see what he says.

Does he get really excited and say yes! That's something I have always wanted to do!

Then you can follow it up with a simple invitation, "Well, hey, let's go do it. What day works best for you?"

The beauty of this approach is this, this is all done on your terms, this is all done when you are ready, and this is done when you have had a chance to see who he is as a person. There are no misleading or false expectations because there is no pressure. **You can have multiple men as friends with no bad feelings because you are not dating anyone.**

This way, you only date men who have already proved themselves to you, that they make good friend material.

And who better to have a relationship with than a best friend?

But you must go into this with the full intention of honestly wanting to expand your social circle and make new friends.

This also serves another purpose. This keeps you busy, so you are not over-investing in someone. This will heal the loneliness that you might be feeling or experiencing.

Know that when you meet a man and decide to take it to the next level, it comes from a place of you being whole and not in pieces. You are coming from a place of **ALREADY** feeling fulfilled, happy, and more grounded in your life, not from a place of needing or fixing something missing from within you.

And another great by-product of expanding your social circle is you will probably come across some pretty cool women who would also make good friends!

Now I know what you are thinking, Kevin, friends? Who wants to be in the friend zone?

Well, let me let you in on another little secret.

Girls, friend zone, guys. So, yes, it is true. Guys generally have a very difficult time getting out of the friend zone.

But guys? Guys typically do not friend zone girls.

Guys who, over time, have become your friend. Are interested.

So, how do you make the transition from "friend" to romantic interest?

Wear something different. Wear an incredible outfit, which makes him go wow!

Be **BOLD** and brave. Men love confidence as much as you do! Bat those lashes, use your charm, be soft and inviting, use your femininity, smile, and be playful!

And then be **BOLD** and invite him over for dinner.

Remember, be soft, inviting, and warm.

Get close to him. Get directly across from him, look deeply in his eyes and say,

"Would you like to come over for dinner this weekend?"

CHAPTER 15:
YOUR IDEAL MAN IS ONLY ONE SMILE AWAY!

INSIDE OUT DATING MAKEOVER

KEVIN BOYLE

As you probably well know by now, when you first see that irresistible hunk standing in line at Starbucks waiting for a coffee, you only have seconds to make a first good impression.

And it's so much easier to make that great first impression if you are already glowing from the inside out (SMILING), have practiced your flirting skills, and are clear about your intention!

Your intention should always be first and foremost. How can I create an opportunity for conversation? That's it! **All you want to do is start a conversation,** and this is the important part. **Is he showing interest?**

Because if his back is to you, or he's looking down at his phone. It's what is called a cold approach. Without some kind of go signal from him, like a smile for example. You do not have permission to approach, and there is a very good chance that you are going to get shot down.

So, always look for some sort of confirmation from him that he is approachable, and that he has given you the green light.

And when he has. Smile, catch his eye, and whisper the words Hi.

Leave no doubt in his mind that you are approachable and interested.

Then look away and walk to a place where he can engage with you, where he can have a conversation with you, away from your friends.

While you are walking to that place, look behind you to see if he is still looking at you, smile again, look down, and brush your hair to the side.

If he doesn't come after you, he is either uninterested or might already be seeing someone else.

Or, you can be BOLD, be courageous, and go for it!

How to approach, and what to say.

You: "Now that's what I like to see in a man."

Him: oh yah, what's that?

Pause, look him right in the eye, grin, and be playful and fun.

You: "A man who…insert a compliment".

And then see how open he is to having a conversation.

Now I know what you are saying, Kevin. I can never do that!

Did you know that 90% of men like it when a woman approaches them?

It takes a lot of pressure off of them.

What I always suggest to women is this. **Practice, practice, practice!**

Practice walking up to strangers and saying;

"Now that's what I like to see…" and practice picking out something nice to compliment them on.

"Someone with great taste in shoes!"

"A man who knows how to handle a grill!"

Everyone loves compliments, especially when they are unexpected. It pulls them out of their world and into yours, and watch their faces light up! You will be amazed at how easy this is and how you will make someone's day! Have fun with it.

Over time you will become more comfortable speaking with and approaching all people, not just people you are interested in, and then one day, it will happen.

You will conquer your fear of meeting new people, you will quiet that tiny little doubting self-conscious voice that we all have, and slowly over time, you will conquer if not minimize your fear of rejection.

Because when you approach people with a compliment, you are not asking them for anything, and who doesn't like a well-intentioned compliment?

And then one day, when you feel ready, you can decide to be BOLD.

The BOLD, cheeky approach: There he is. You muster up your courage, walk up to him, and say it.

You: "Now that's what I like to see in a man...." BIG smile, pause, look him in the eye, and follow it up with;

You: "A man with great taste in women...."

Have a good laugh, and then see how open he is to having a conversation.

Or, You: "Excuse me, what's your name?"

Him: It's Jack.

Be cheeky as hell and look him directly in the eyes and say.

You: "Nice to meet you, Jack. I am going to let Santa know exactly what I want for Christmas this year."

Have a good laugh, and then see how open he is to having a conversation.

Men like playful, flirty, **and DIRECT!**

You: "So now that you know how absolutely amazing I am. Are you going to ask me for my number?"

CHAPTER 16:
GETTING READY FOR YOUR FIRST DATE. THE TEN CRITICAL FIRST DATE RULES!

INSIDE OUT DATING MAKEOVER

KEVIN BOYLE

1. Go for coffee, a drink, or a walk… not dinner, and no Netflix and Chills.
2. Wear something pretty & subtle. It should NOT be your best/sexiest outfit.
3. Save that for another date. Make it so he is dating you because he likes YOU, not because of your "packaging."
4. Use your own transportation to get to and from the date.
5. Do not share too much personal information with a man you have just met – i.e., where you live / past relationships.
6. A planner, not a player, offers and pays for the first date (it is polite for you to offer to pay for half FIRST). These small gestures are how you set yourself apart from your competition. Remember, you want to be completely different from any other woman he has ever met or dated.
7. **Wait for him to call you for a 2nd date.** Do not obsess about him, you do not know him well enough to be thinking about wedding bells and the names of your first four children. So do not call him, do not text him, and go live your life!
8. If he is serious about you, he will call you for another date within a week of meeting you.
9. DO NOT speak poorly of men, your experiences with dating, relationships, or your ex.
10. If he asks you out and you are busy that day - **offer him an alternative -** "oh dam, I'd love to get together, but I am busy

that night - how about next Thursday instead?" No man wants to be seen as clingy or a stalker, so if you say you are busy, most men will assume you're just not that interested.

If he asks you what you are looking for;

You: "I am definitely not looking to get married anytime soon, but I am not looking for anything casual either. I would like to think I take a pretty healthy approach to dating. I would say I am somewhere in the middle."

"But I will tell you this. What I have learned about men is that when a man finds the right woman, the woman he knows he wants to be with, he will do everything RIGHT to win her over because he doesn't ever want to risk losing her."

CHAPTER 17:
THE TEN BEST FIRST DATE QUESTIONS!

INSIDE OUT DATING MAKEOVER

KEVIN BOYLE

The first date should be light, fun, and involve some casual flirting!

Men are very visual. We LOVE cheeky. So let your playfulness speak for you!

Risk being vulnerable. Risk being a little bit awkward and dorky. Over time, with practice, you will become super sexy and super attractive to men.

While on the date, try not to ask too many fact-based questions. To a man, it feels like an interview or worse, like an interrogation, and quite honestly, most of the time, it feels like you have an "agenda," which feels like pressure to a man.

Some examples of great first date questions:

1. So, what do you like to do for fun, and how do you like to spend your weekends?
2. What's your favorite childhood memory?
3. Looking back on your life, what's been your highest high?
4. If you had a time machine, what time period would you go to?
5. If you could be famous, what would you want to be known for?
6. What do you think about the statement that beside every great man is a great woman? Pause, let him answer… Follow Up; What makes a woman great to you?
7. If you were ruler of the world for one day, what would you do?
8. What are some of the most amazing adventures you have ever been on, or what is the craziest thing you've ever done?
9. What is next on your bucket list?

Risking vulnerability near the end of the date:

This is your time to be vulnerable. This is your time to be unlike any other woman he has ever dated before. This is your time to RISK rejection, **but isn't it better to know now** rather than spend the next five days wondering if he is going to call you or not?

10. "I had so much fun tonight, so yes, I would definitely LOVE to see you again! Carl, I am curious, where are you at in your dating life right now, what are you looking for?

Does he act casual and nonchalant? "Well, I don't like to put labels on things. I am kind of a free spirit. I just like to take things casual (not a good answer, code for; easy sex with no investment and no commitment).

Does he act evasively? Because he wants your answer before he answers. "Well, what do you mean?" (not a good answer, he knows exactly what you mean), or does he turn the question back on you by asking you what do you want in a relationship or where are you at in your dating life?

And if everything goes well?

Classy end-of-date move, (softly touch wrist, arm, or shoulder);

Lean in and kiss him lightly on the cheek.

Inside he will be melting, and he will only be thinking, when can I see this girl again?

Men like BOLD, confident women who know how to get what they want!

CHAPTER 18:
SIGNS THAT HE IS A PLAYER...

INSIDE OUT DATING MAKEOVER

KEVIN BOYLE

Intention is an amazing tool.

Anyone who is serious about you is not going to leave any doubt in your mind about his intentions.

Why? Because he does not want to run the risk of you going out on a date with someone else on a Friday or Saturday night. He will call you well before the weekend to ensure that he gets to see you and spend time with you.

- He won't talk about where the relationship is headed.
- When you return his calls, often, he does not pick up.
- On weekends, he is not available, or he seems like he is always really busy.
- Always pay in cash.
- The phone is always face down, so you can't see any text messages that might come in.
- Often waits until the very last minute (Thursday / Friday) to ask you out for the weekend. Revealing that you might be his "plan b" girl.
- He does not proactively call you to show interest in getting to know you.
- He says he's not ready for anything serious…

You say: "That's fine, but I want someone on the same page as me, so I think it's best we go our separate ways. So, let's just get the check, and don't worry, I'll pay for my half."

Him: No, no baby, you misunderstood me, I'm just playing, I really like you…

You: But that's the point, you are playing, and I am not.

- He checks out other women while he is out with you / is overly flirtatious with the female wait staff.

- Has he never introduced you to his friends and/or family even though you have been dating for months.

- Does he introduce sex as a topic into your conversation on the first date?

- Is he overly "touchy-feely" on the first date?

- There are long gaps between when you hear from him.

CHAPTER 19:
AFTER THE DATE, YOUR POST DATE CHECK-IN.

INSIDE OUT DATING MAKEOVER

KEVIN BOYLE

On reflecting on your date, the SINGLE most important question you need to ask yourself is this...

How does he TRY to make me feel about myself when I am around him?

Because if he's trying to make you feel bad, small, or insecure about yourself in any way, you have to ask yourself, is that a battle I want to have every single day, and with every single interaction I have with him, **and more importantly, why do I think he is trying to make me feel bad about myself?**

- Did he dimmish me in any way?
- Did he make any off-handed remarks about my appearance?
- Did he make me feel self-conscious about my age, my looks, etc.?
- Do I feel like I am not good enough?
- Do I feel like I need to prove myself worthy of him?
- **Did he treat me with respect?**

Because it doesn't matter how cute or handsome he is, it doesn't matter how funny or charming he is, it doesn't matter what he does, how much money he makes, or what kind of car he drives.

None of these matter if he does not treat you with respect!

- How did he react when I expressed my boundaries?
- Do I feel like I need to change my standards or my boundaries if I want to be with him?

These are ALL Red Flags – and should rule out a second date.

My best piece of advice for you is to **TRUST your GUT!**

"Our gut" or intuition is that inner voice we all have that guides and supports us throughout our lives. According to researchers at Leeds University, intuition is a psychological process in which the brain makes decisions based on our past experiences while taking cues from our immediate environment.

The best way to access your intuition is to;

a) Make sure you are in a quiet place and then meditate on the decision that you are about to make.

b) Take time to listen to your whole body. Intuition reveals itself to us as a feeling within us.

c) Then ask yourself the question, does your intuition feel expansive or contractive?

If the sensation you are feeling is tight, clenched, or a sense of foreboding. This indicates a big no to whatever you are thinking about doing. Know that if you ignore what your gut is trying to tell you, there is a good chance that your relationship with him will be difficult and most likely full of drama.

Meanwhile, a feeling of lightness, openness, and energy, even when accompanied by fear, suggests you should move forward with your decision.

After you check how you feel when you are around him, you should ask yourself the following question… **Am I more attracted to his looks, personality, or character?**

Because if you choose to ignore your gut, your relationship with him will always be difficult and full of drama, and over time you will start to secretly hate yourself for choosing to invest your time and your emotions in someone that you know is not right for you and at the same time, you will slowly start to resent him, for being him.

After you check how you feel when you are around him, you need to ask yourself…

- Was he a gentleman during the date?
- Does he willingly pay for the date?
- Does he open doors for you?
- Is he polite to the people around him, like the wait staff?
- How does he speak about others, about exes?
- Does he seem to respect my opinion?
- How long does he wait to call before the next date?
- Does he take the time to call me and get to know me?
- Is he a planner? What are his goals in life?

CHAPTER 20:
KEVIN, WHAT ARE SOME BASIC RULES FOR SETTING BETTER BOUNDARIES AND STANDARDS WITH MEN?

INSIDE OUT DATING MAKEOVER

KEVIN BOYLE

- No Netflix and Chill dates until you are ready to be intimate. (because, in my opinion, when someone says "Netflix and Chill," this is code for "I want to have sex with you.")
- Do not date a man who calls you names or diminishes you in any way. Does he call women bitches or hoes? Tell him how uncomfortable it makes you feel and see if his behavior changes. If it doesn't, drop him.
- Is he jealous, angry, or possessive for no reason? Have a conversation with him and ask if he would consider getting help. If not, drop him.
- Do I feel a strong desire to help him? (Code for "fix" him). People need to figure out their own lives. You cannot save someone from themselves.
- Does he treat you with respect, does he listen to you, and do you have an equal voice in your relationship?
- Do not chase men! Do not text him first, do not call him first. Men go hard for what they say they want, and if a man is not investing time into you and your relationship, **you are not what he wants.** Most likely, you are a placeholder until something better comes along.

Note: I know it is very hard to feel like you are sitting by the phone waiting for him to call (or text). This is why it is so critically important for you to have a life outside of him. Asking him to pursue is the only reliable way I know of for you to gauge his level of interest.

- It is ok for you to say no to him. Does he respect your boundaries?
- Is he best friend material?
- Would I be proud to introduce him to my father, mom, friends, and family?

CHAPTER 21:
FAQ

INSIDE OUT DATING MAKEOVER

KEVIN BOYLE

* Kevin, seriously, what is the point of doing all of this work??? Every guy I meet is either a jerk, a user, only interested in sex, or emotionally unavailable!

This is exactly the reason why you need to do the work!

Your life is only a reflection of who you are being, who you think you are, and who you think you deserve.

It's the universal law of attraction at work that states;

"We do not experience things as they are. **We experience things as we are."**

Because, yes, I am making **the very strong argument** that life is so much easier with **a good man** beside you sharing life's challenges and responsibilities.

Trust me, seriously, do the work and **follow the tips and strategies in this book**. Your life will change, and you will experience a powerful inside-out, life-changing TRANSFORMATION!

And you will experience men; differently, I promise!

* But Kevin, I am too old, ugly, (etc.) no one wants me!

Actually, I am very happy to tell you that you are quite mistaken, many of my best clients are 45, 50, 55 and my oldest client to date is 60 years young!

Yes, while it is true most men prefer younger women. **As a man matures, his taste in women evolves,** and he becomes more reasonable in his expectations of who he wants to share his life with.

Follow the seven steps of your inside-out dating makeover (starting on page 90) and be unlike any other woman he has ever met in his life before, and you will completely BLOW his mind, **regardless of your age!**

He will think to himself, my god, how refreshing! This is the kind of woman I have always wanted to meet, my dream girl! And if you follow the steps, it will happen faster than you think!

* Kevin, can you help me with my online dating profile?

Sure, here's a great headline you can steal from me.

Day 1,226 of being on an online dating app and why I think I'll just get a cat instead.

That pretty well sums up my thoughts on online dating. I honestly cannot think of one positive thing to say about online dating.

Except that it is "easy," and that's the problem.

I think online dating and social media have almost destroyed modern dating and relationships.

Essentially online dating has become a game of, are you "hot or not," **where appearance takes precedence over personality and character** and where most people are treated like disposable objects.

And yes, I know, you will tell me about the one friend you have or your cousin who met the love of their life on an online dating app. I agree it can happen, but those are few and far between. The vast majority of people do not find success on online dating platforms unless they are looking for casual sex and easy hook-ups.

So, yes, you can try and find a good high-quality man through online dating.

But let me warn you, it is like trying to find a needle in a haystack. The most recent studies of what percentage of women find successful long-term relationships from online dating, depending on which source you read, is anywhere from 3 to 11%.

You need to kiss a lot of "frogs" to make online dating work, and during that time, it can damage you a lot. When you kiss that many frogs, over time, you can become disillusioned, frustrated, untrusting, and jaded.

Having given you my thoughts on online dating, I also know it is a reality. So, I suggest that if you are meeting men online, you have the following conversation with them before meeting them live and in person.

The questions you SHOULD be asking men you have met online before you agree to a first date! (preferably, in a phone conversation)

For example:

He calls you… Hey Chiara – how are you doing?

You: I am great, thanks! I just finished watching a fantastic new Netflix documentary!

Him: Oh really? Which one is that?

You: Pick a cause you care about… and see what he says; for example, if you care about "climate change."

Him: Oh, climate change – you know I don't know much about that…

You: No problem! I am just curious, what are some of your pet causes? What are the things that you really care about?

Him: Actually, I am a big brother. I have been volunteering with Big Brother for over ten years now.

You: Oh, that's really cool. I really like community-minded people.

You: How did you get involved with Big Brother?

Him: I just really like kids.

You: Oh, that's awesome! So, do I! So, what do you like to do for fun when you are not working or volunteering with Big Brother?

Him: I like to workout, go to movies, comedy clubs – those kinds of things.

You: I love comedy clubs! One of the things I am actually looking for is someone **to share some fun weekend adventures with.**

You: **"Tell me, I am just curious, where are you in your dating life right now? Are your weekends generally free for dating?"**

Him: I am definitely looking for something serious, but I do work a lot… (which is usually code for I am married or I am dating a lot of girls).

Him: I don't really have time for dating and getting to know someone like most people, you know? I was just hoping that tomorrow night, I have some time. Maybe we could Netflix and Chill?

Him: You know I really like you. You are so beautiful, and you are not like most of the other girls I have talked to on this site.

You: Yah, Chad, I am sorry that's not going to work for me. A man married to his job has no time for a social life or time to get to know me. It's just not going to work.

Know your value, your boundaries, your standards, know the red flags (works a lot), and do not make any exceptions for anyone.

* What to text him when he texts you, "Hey" or "Hey Stranger," etc.

The Cheeky response;

You: "Hey is for horses. Are you saying I look like a horse???"

The general rule of texting is to put the same effort into your responses as he is putting into his PMs.

But I'll be super honest with you, if he's putting this much effort into a text with you, it's not going anywhere.

You get what you are willing to accept.

Forget about him, and go find someone else who is worthy of you. A man who can form complete sentences.

Remember: Hire slow, fire FAST!

* How to respond to men who "neg" you (say things to try and diminish you) or to "mean girls" who are trying to bully you.

You: Nonchalant as hell; "And I would care, why?" then turn your back and walk away.

* When he contacts you for a last-minute date.

Be very careful about accepting last-minute dates even if you are free. You may be his plan B girl.

Generally speaking, someone who is serious about you and who really likes you is going to call you early in the week to ask you out because;

He does not want to leave any doubt about his wanting to see you and his wanting to get to know you better, and secondly and most importantly, he is not going to want to risk you going out on a date with someone else.

* I haven't heard from him in over a week. Should I worry?

When it comes to men, dating, and relationships, this is the one critically important thing you need to know about men;

If he wanted to, he would.

If you have to ask a man; so, what are we, why haven't you called, or where is this relationship going?

The answer is nowhere.

Men, by nature, are hunters and go for what they want. He will push through and overcome anything to be with you if you are the one.

Do not make the mistake of making it any more complicated than that.

Action Plan: Forget about him, and go find someone else who is into you.

* Why does he pull away when you feel like the two of you are just starting to get close?

He is either spinning more than one plate (seeing other girls), or he could be emotionally damaged. You might be starting to touch on his wounds, and because he cannot handle true intimacy, he needs to create distance between you and him to regain "control," or he's been lying to you, and things were great as long as the two of you were not serious.

Most likely, he either doesn't want you the same way you want him, he is wounded or damaged from something that happened to him in the past, he simply is not ready for a serious relationship with you, or he is married.

Remember when a guy really likes you, and he is emotionally available for you, he will do everything right because he does not want to ever risk losing you.

When I was dating, I always kept in mind that. **No answer is an answer.**

If he can't slay his inner demons to be with you, if he can't or won't get the help he needs to be with you. What do you think your marriage after you have a baby with him is going to look like?

You need to catch this early because if you ever decide to have children with him, you need to make sure he is "in" for the long haul and that he can be a responsible husband and father.

But here is another thing that I have learned about human behavior after working with clients.

His losing you completely is the only way you are going to motivate him to change and get serious about you. People have to lose something first before they see the value in it.

But if and when he comes back to you, if you are willing to take him back. You need to insist that he goes and gets counseling. He must sort out himself if he ever wants to win you back. You do not need to be his yo-yo girl because of what is happening inside of him!

* Is it true that all men just want sex?

Well, as it turns out, no. In a recent study by a leading online dating magazine of over 10,000 single men. Men were asked,

"What do you want most out of your love life?"

86% of single men who took the poll responded that they are looking to find and fall in love with the woman of their dreams.

Huh? What? Then how come every single guy I meet seems to only want sex?

Well, the answer is yes and no. Yes, all men want sex, **but not all men push for it.**

In fact, if a guy really likes you, most men will usually wait until you are ready.

If he does not or he won't, he might be just too immature for you or more than likely he is just not ready to settle down yet, and he is still "playing the field."

So, more often than not, it all depends on **where and how you are meeting men**.

If you are online, the vast majority of men are online looking for sex. So, it stands to reason that you would start to believe that the majority of men are only interested in sex.

If you are meeting men in clubs and bars, guess what? The vast majority of men in clubs and bars are looking for sex.

If you get cold approached a lot, and you love a guy who exudes confidence, who is charming and smooth as ice, guess what? The vast majority of men who cold approach women are pick-up artists looking for sex.

If you are attracted to the "bad boys," the "Chad's and the Tyrone's," the types of guys who are used to tons of women throwing themselves at them, and the cost of admission to date them is sex. Then you guessed it, you will start to believe over time that that is the only way you can get a man and that all men are interested in is sex.

The truth is that the vast majority of men who are online rarely get a response and rarely get a date. Most single men in bars don't even get a chance to speak to a woman. Most men are too afraid of rejection to ever cold approach a woman, and lastly, most men can only dream of ever living the life of a bad boy, a Chad or a Tyrone.

The simple truth is that most men are just regular guys looking for a good woman to settle down with and make a life with.

*** Kevin, what do you think is the most important quality for me to look for in a man if I am marriage minded and if I want to have children one day?**

Finding the right man like I said earlier, is quite difficult for women for a lot of very different reasons. That's why it's not really about one thing, there are so many different qualities you need to be on the lookout for.

But as you are dating a man, I think you should ask yourself this one question.

Is he good husband material, and will he make a good father to my children?

A good husband, in my opinion, treats you with respect, is competent, and is responsible. Everything else, like whether he is taller than you, handsome or not, or whether you have anything in common, from my experience, is just "icing on the cake."

For example. Anyone who knows my wife and I, knows that Maggie and I have very little in common. She is a practicing Catholic, I am not. She loves to ski, I love to dance. And yet despite having so little in common, we still have an amazing relationship!

* When he pushes for sex too soon;

You: "As much as I like you, I am not quite ready to be your girlfriend just yet."

When he is very aggressive with sex;

You: "Whoa Tiger! You need to stop!" "I am not sure where you learned this Joe, but this makes me feel very unsafe."

Now, this is the most important part. **How does he REACT** to you setting your boundaries?

Sulky, mad, pleading, laying down ultimatums, or does he ignore your boundaries and continue on anyway?

These are all red flags and, worse, manipulations. Do you really want to be with a guy who does not respect where you are in the relationship and what you want?

He reacted the wrong way.

You: Actually, I hate to do this right now, but I have to go anyway, it's getting late, and I have some things I need to do early tomorrow morning.

He reacted the right way.

Him: ok, sorry, I just got carried away.

You: ok, np, just so you know, I do not sleep with a man unless we are boyfriend, or girlfriend. And in order for me to be your girlfriend, I have to feel super comfortable with you, and I have to know we are both on the same page.

* Help Kevin, I think I am being "love bombed!"

Being love-bombed is another form of manipulation or, worse yet, an indication that this man who is so crazy about you that hardly knows anything about you could very well be a narcissist.

Think about it.

Texting and calling every day. When you first start dating? Yes, it is very flattering, but in my opinion, more often than not, it is a red flag. Because love bombing is not in most men's true nature. Most men's true nature is that they value their space and freedom. That's why men have "man caves." That's why most men love to go off on their own and tinker, work on their cars, or on their hobbies.

If you are being love-bombed, you are generally either dealing with a player trying to get into your pants as quickly as possible or with a narcissist.

Watch for controlling behavior as your relationship moves forward; Where were you last night? Who was that guy you were just talking to?

* Ok, Kevin, I know you said not to give out my number to anyone who cold approaches me, but this guy is soooooo CUTE!

Listen, don't say I didn't warn yah, but ok. Who am I to stand in your way of fairy tales, a lifetime of crushed dreams and train wrecks.

When he asks you for your number:

You: "Sure, but first I need to know if you are single or not?"

Him: oh yeah, I am single.

You: "So, there's no one out there that might think they're in a relationship with you?" Quickly followed up with;

You are incredulous: **"How does someone like you not have any girlfriends?"**

Him: ok, ok, but it's complicated…

You: "Sorry, I don't do "complicated."

CHAPTER 22:
THE TEN QUESTIONS YOU NEED TO ANSWER BEFORE HAVING SEX WITH A MAN.

INSIDE OUT DATING MAKEOVER

KEVIN BOYLE

1. Check your investment level; It's not JUST about how you feel about him. **A man's value to you should ONLY be based on how well he treats you**, not by how much he says he loves you, likes you, or what he "has."
2. Does he push for sex or make declarations around when you should have sex (like the 3-date rule), or that he will commit to you only when you have had sex with him?
3. Does he try to have sex with you without a condom or discussing birth control?
4. **CONSISTENCY**; Is he calling, and are you going out on dates at least once a week in order for the two of you to get to know each other better?
5. Is he a workaholic? Does he use work or school as an excuse for not calling or making time to see you?
6. How does he react when you give him boundaries? Badly, upset, or indignant?
7. Are his first, second, or third date suggestions, Netflix and Chill?
8. Have you had the **"Is he willing, and is he able to have deep, meaningful conversations that matter?"** conversation with him? (found on page 159).
9. How did he react when you opened yourself up to him, and you showed your soft, vulnerable side? Supportive, relaxed, and with empathy?
10. How do you really feel when you are with him? **Do you feel good, relaxed, trusting, and genuinely happy,** or do you feel insecure, needy, unsure if he likes you or not, or unsupported?

CHAPTER 23:
GETTING TO COMMITMENT; THE FIVE STEPS TO GETTING HIM TO WANT TO COMMIT! ACTIVATE YOUR SUPERPOWER; FEMININITY!

INSIDE OUT DATING MAKEOVER

KEVIN BOYLE

If you are not having success with men, dating, and relationships. This is usually one of the MAJOR missing pieces of the puzzle.

Femininity is what men are looking for in a woman, and **it is what men CRAVE.**

Femininity is your SUPERPOWER.

The Queen is the MOST powerful piece on the board when she learns how to use her power properly. Knowing that men will move mountains for a truly feminine woman.

But femininity REQUIRES something of you.

Femininity requires you to be vulnerable.

And not every woman is willing to truly risk being vulnerable to a man.

It's just too scary.

But for the woman who can step through her fears and insecurities and embrace her femininity, the rewards are WELL worth it.

Because a truly feminine woman can and will get whatever she wants out of life. She will get the man she wants, and she will get the relationship that she wants.

For the woman who is sick and tired of mixed and confusing messages from men, players wasting her time, emotionally unavailable men, and men unwilling or unable to commit.

Vulnerability is the antidote.

For the woman who wonders why men do not stick around, why she rarely gets second dates, or why men ghost her.

Vulnerability is the antidote.

Vulnerability is the key to how approachable you are.

It is the key to how playful and how sexy you are.

It is the key to experiencing genuine heartfelt connection, which leads to deep, meaningful conversations with men.

It is the key to allowing men to show up in your life as heroes instead of villains.

And ultimately, it is the key to unlocking his heart.

If you really are serious about getting out of your own way when it comes to finding the most amazing man of your dreams and having the most amazing relationship of your dreams, you need to conquer your fears, risk being seen, and risk being vulnerable.

Tips on activating your SUPERPOWER and being more feminine;

- Don't ever forget, the BEST accessory you can ever wear when you go out is your SMILE!
- Be soft, warm, inviting, cheeky, playful, and fun!
- Take care of how you look and your hygiene.
- Dress appropriately when on dates. Pretty dresses, skirts, and heels.
- Longer hair is typically more feminine and more preferred by men.
- Be flirtatious, SMILE, and make eye contact.
- When you are out and about and walking with him, lean into his shoulder. He probably won't say anything. He will be too busy thinking about how lucky he is to have someone like you, so warm, cuddly, and feminine.

And when he looks at you, look at him and smile. Inside he will be melting!

- Touching, when he passes by you or you pass by him, a soft touch is all it takes to connect with him.
- Cultivate good manners and proper etiquette.
- Ditch the swear words, ghetto lingo, and crude language.
- And lastly, and **most importantly, be vulnerable!**

CHAPTER 24:
DO YOU KNOW HOW TO BE A CHALLENGE AND HOW TO BE FUN AND FLIRTY AT THE SAME TIME?

INSIDE OUT DATING MAKEOVER

KEVIN BOYLE

The challenge for men is to swallow their pride, set aside their ego, and risk rejection when he approaches you, and when he asks you out on those first few dates.

The challenge for women is to drop this idea that you have to be "perfect" and that you don't "need" a man. Because being "perfect" and "having 20-foot high walls up around you" scares men away. What man wants to be with a woman who is not showing any excitement or interest in being with him?

If men with all of their fears and all of their insecurities are willing to risk rejection to man up and come meet you and ultimately be with you.

Then you, as a woman with all of your fears and insecurities, should strongly consider being willing to embrace your femininity and risk being vulnerable.

Why?

One of the many reasons why so many women choose the bad boy is because they are not willing to risk being truly vulnerable around men.

So often, women choose men where they do not have to risk anything, and because they are not willing to risk anything, they don't have to bother setting up and maintaining standards with men.

Because if there is ONE thing that will scare away a "bad" boy, it's when you are being vulnerable.

When you are with a bad boy, someone who doesn't ever want anything from you, he doesn't care about you, he hasn't put you up on a pedestal, and more importantly, **he never wants to have a conversation with you about anything that matters.**

When you choose bad boys, you never have to risk being truly vulnerable with a man because, let's be completely honest, being vulnerable with a man probably scares the heck out of you.

So, if a man is willing to risk rejection, you need to risk being vulnerable.

You need to risk being seen as human, with faults and imperfections. That is the risk of rejection that you need to take. Because men have this ideal of women, they tend to put women up on pedestals. Society teaches men to "always be a gentleman" and to put women first. **He is only doing what he has been conditioned** and told to do.

And when he does what he has been conditioned to do, you friend zone him.

The only thing stopping you from meeting the "good" ones is your unwillingness to be vulnerable.

So, you need to get real and **ask yourself why are you resisting?**

Because if you are not willing to be vulnerable with him, it's going to be very hard for you to be playful, which is a key component of attraction.

If you are not willing to be vulnerable, it's going to be very hard for you to have deep, meaningful conversations that get you to the connection you say you want with men.

If you are not willing to be vulnerable, it's virtually impossible for him to show up for you in the way he wants and needs to, which is as your hero.

You need to ask yourself.

Why are you getting in your own way of having the kind of man and the kind of relationship you say you want?

Pride, EGO, fear, insecurity, unhealed wounds, fear of rejection, and a willingness to be truly vulnerable with a man.

All that stands between you and having the most amazing relationship of your life!

The dos and don'ts of flirting and texting.

Let's address one of the biggest reasons (there are others, but let's just deal with this one for now) why most men do not call you back for a second date.

Your fears about and around SEX.

You are so afraid that if you flirt with a man, he will get the wrong idea, so you present yourself as either cold, uninviting, uninterested in him or sex, or worse, as boring!

He wants to know how playful you are, he wants to know that there is a naughty side to you, he wants a "taste" of what it is like to be with you, and he wants to feel that tension.

The tension that comes from you setting and maintaining standards and boundaries. The tension that comes from the push and pull of attraction. One minute you are soft, feminine, and wanting. The next, playfully pushing him away. It is a dance.

He wants to know how completely different you are from any other girl he has ever dated!

So, the one-million-dollar question becomes.

How do you let a man know you are sexual without being sexual?

The BIG THREE; **Femininity, playfulness, and maintaining your boundaries** in your flirting, texting, and interactions with him.

Femininity: Are you dressed the part? Pretty dress, heels, appropriate makeup. Your demeanor is soft, warm, and inviting. Big smiles, joyous laughter, and lots of flirty eye contact.

Playfulness. Your willingness to tease him and be cheeky in a very fun way.

Boundaries: are where the sexual tension and attraction come from. Men, despite their protests, love boundaries, and they love to push them.

Because when you "play it safe," or worse, "playing almost impossible to get," you are not fun, you are not exciting, you are not someone he looks forward to talking to, to ever seeing again, and I hate to break it to you, you are probably coming off as quite standoffish or boring.

Sure, if he's got no game, he might settle for you, but would you settle?

So, first of all, do not go overboard. If you over-invest in a guy too quickly, he will lose interest. You want **to act like you like him**, but not like you have both of your futures already planned out.

Act like I like him? Uhhhh, Kevin, that is the complete opposite of what I have been told by almost EVERY dating coach, relationship expert, or guru.

Yeah, and they are all single, or they have been married and divorced five times.

But Kevin, seriously, if I act like I like him, **won't I just scare him away?**

Yes, if he's the wrong guy, you might. But isn't that what you want? To stop wasting your time on men who are players, users only interested in sex, emotionally unavailable men, and men who are not ready or willing to ever commit because they have never done the work. Because they are probably damaged or wounded in some way?

But also keep in mind, I am asking you to "act" like you like him, **not tell him** that you like him. There is a big difference. If you are acting like you like him, but you are not putting it into words. He's most likely going to be thinking, she's acting like she likes me, but I am still not 100% sure.

Ok, that makes sense. So, Kevin, why can't I just tell him the "truth" then? That I am looking for a serious relationship, that I want to get married one day and have a family?

Why not just be "straight up with men?"

As mentioned earlier, at the end of your first date, tell him whether you would like to see him again or not. And then ask him about his dating intentions. Don't worry, **you will have your answer in his response.**

But there is another reason, one that is much more subtle. When you are "screening" men for future potential, you want to come from a place of abundance. You want to come from a place of "having" instead of a place of "getting." Not from a place of wanting or needing.

Remember, the universe only **gives you more of who you are being.**

If you are asking, you "do not have."

And more importantly, if you are asking, you are "trying to get."

In the same way, if you are "playing hard to get" while dating a man, it only **sends him the message** that **you are not interested.**

So, the universe only **gives you even more of who you are being.**

Which is someone who is "uninterested in men."

Why, as a man looking for a relationship, would I waste any more of my time pursuing a woman who is not showing any interest in me?

My wife, who I am madly in love with, let me know on the first date that she was into me. There was no doubt in my mind.

She flirted with me the whole date, we laughed, we had fun, and she would "push" me away in a very; "I like you, but I am not easy" cheeky, playful kind of way.

Men love the push-pull. Imagine a rubber band. Walk towards him, laughing, smiling, then playfully push him away and say, "You are definitely not my type."

And Magdalena COMPLETELY won me over.

So refreshing and different from almost every other woman I had ever dated!

Everything just flowed, we had a vibe, and I loved it!

And then, at the end of the date, she told me she would love to see me again.

She completely BLEW my mind, and then **Magdalena did the unthinkable!**

She asked me for a second date at the end of our first date.

Yes, that's right. **We went out on two dates that night.** Two different locations and we spent a total of four hours together that night having a BLAST! (most dating gurus, books, etc., suggest only one hour max on your first date).

Femininity, playfulness, and maintaining your standards and your boundaries.

Be the MOST amazing woman of his dreams. GIVE him the experience that he has always CRAVED. BE the woman he has always wanted. BE unlike any other woman he has ever dated in his life! BE his Mount Everest, and be the only mountain he ever wants to climb!

What kind of texts and dm's are ok to send?

Most women assume that all men only want to see dirty pictures of you.

Some women think that because men have such sexually driven minds that we want you to be dirty and raunchy. We don't. Most men like playfulness, teasing, and a little bit of mystery.

It's the same as the way you dress for your dates. Wear form-fitting, flattering clothes that leave something to the imagination.

Rule #1 of sending texts and DMs.

NEVER send a man a picture of you nude. Whether you are in a serious long-term relationship with a man or just met him and you just started dating.

What if you guys, for whatever reason, break up?

What if it's messy, and he gets mad at you and wants revenge?

What do you think is going to happen with those nude photos of you?

Instead, be playful and fun, and feed his imagination.

Men love the thought of POSSIBILITY. A good text should tease him in a very light, fun, playful way. Let's face it, a man's sex drive is the fast lane to his heart.

Knowing what to text and how to text him is a good way to light the fires of passion in him for you.

Your text should stick in his mind along with his thoughts of you and create desire!

Build tension and keep it mysterious by giving him a glimpse of what you have to offer, and let his imagination do the rest of the "work."

But, DON'T send too much. You do not want to send him too many flirty texts all at once.

You want to offer him a "glimpse" of what you have in store for him. Don't give him too much, and don't give him too much at once.

Because there is a real risk, you will be seen as too eager.

And "too eager," too soon, KILLS attraction.

Examples of some fun, flirty, playful texts or things to say:

Do you want to be that sexy, confident woman that every man finds absolutely irresistible?

The type of woman that climbs deep inside a man's mind and never leaves?

BE the woman he has always dreamed of, be unlike any other woman he has ever dated. Because it's time to be the woman that he has always craved!

Most women think that most guys just want sex. But just like you, most guys are looking for a woman who is willing to go on an adventure, someone who, in their day-to-day life, is fun!

Most women, when texting or flirting, make the very common mistake of responding with "boring," mindless "hey, how are you doing…", and way too many emojis and LOLs.

Why not say something playful, "teasing," and flirtatious? Something that makes you IRRESISTIBLE in his mind!

This is your chance to be different. This is your chance to really engage a man at a core level that will leave him craving for more… more of you, and only you!

Putting it in action:

Important Note! Do not overuse and do not use all of these at once. It's always best to follow the golden rule of dating "more often than not, less is more." You do not want to seem over eager. Below are some suggestions. Pick the ones you feel most comfortable with!

After you have been on a fantastic date **and he texts you**, you can start off your text by saying, "Well, hello handsome…"

Wait a few seconds, then send a new message, "I am still wearing that smile you gave me last night."

How to ask him out: Hey, my friends and I are going out bowling tomorrow. You can come if you want if you're not afraid of losing to a girl :p

Having conversations: You are so interesting. Tell me all of your stories!

After he says something interesting: lean in, hand on chin, "mmmm, you just might be the most fascinating/handsome/interesting man I have ever met in my entire life!"

Reminiscing: I remember the exact moment when I realized that I wanted to go out with you…

Cheeky: "This is NEVER going to work out… you are way too much work!"

Cheeky and Challenging: "I'll give you a solid 5…"

Him: "oh yah!"

You: "A solid 5 out of 10. You definitely need a lot of work :p."

Always leave him wanting more; Be the first one to stop the kissing. It leaves him wanting more.

CHAPTER 25:
DO YOU HAVE VULNERABLE, HEARTFELT CONVERSATIONS WITH YOUR MAN?

INSIDE OUT DATING MAKEOVER

KEVIN BOYLE

The three-step easy-to-use process for deep, vulnerable conversations with men leads to long-lasting commitment!

A man's role is to maintain a masculine frame. You are not going to like it but think about it. I need you to be really honest with me right now. Do you really respect a man who is a doormat or a pushover?

And if you don't respect a man, are you really sexually attracted to him? I highly doubt it.

So, understand in your communication with him, in your relationship, when you have difficult conversations, there is the Ying and the Yang.

This is not about who is better or less than. This is not about power plays or your submission to men. This is about understanding what attracts you to a man, what makes you want to stay with him, and conversely, what attracts him to a woman and what makes him want to fully commit himself to you even when there is difficulty in your relationship.

Remember when you first started reading this book, and I tried my best to explain the relationship dynamic between men and women.

It's like chess. Men have a strong desire to show competence in order to have their Queen's respect and devotion to him.

The Queen is complimentary. She offers balance, co-operation, and partnership to his masculine energy through her feminine energy.

And in this way, men and women both share a great responsibility.

To be a role model for children in healthy, loving, equal relationships.

And one day, you and your husband will be sitting at the dinner table, surrounded by all of your children and your grandchildren. And you will look deep into your husband's eyes, smile warmly, and say to him, we built this TOGETHER.

As I mentioned earlier, I and many of today's modern men (certainly my male friends) that I speak with **fully support** women working and women's access to equality in the workplace and equal pay for equal work.

But here is where my thoughts differ.

Yes, as a woman, you can focus on your career because, yes, I know you are passionate about your job, passionate about maintaining your independence, and passionate about making sure you can provide for yourself if your marriage should ever fail.

I get it. That kind of thinking is prudent and very smart.

I certainly am encouraging my daughter Chiara to get a good education and a good job, but not at the risk of finding a good man and raising a family.

I think the greatest fear for most women is trusting men.

So instead, you mistakenly put your trust in a job, in a company.

But in doing so, you are only lying to yourself.

The lie of independence.

The reality is that you are not ever truly independent.

Instead of trusting in one man, a man who has taken the time to prove his worth to you, who has taken the time to build a life with you, a man who has taken the time to earn your trust, a man who loves you, you would rather place your trust and be dependant on some faceless, heartless corporation or boss who doesn't care about you and who could and would let you go on a whim.

And you may sit here and think that your career matters. Matters so much that you would risk setting aside your most fertile and desirable years. But the truth is, no matter how hard you work or how much of your life you dedicate to your job or your career, **no one at work will ever truly care about you or love you as much as your man and your children.**

No one.

So, know this, **a life without children, it is an "ok" life.** I get it. It's a choice.

But let me tell you, **before I had my daughter, I was pretty convinced that I never wanted to have children either.** Because I really do care about the planet, and I personally did not want to contribute to overpopulation. And if you were to go back in time and ask me back then if I wanted children, I would have 100% told you no. I don't. I was perfectly "happy" with the thought of never having children.

Fast forward to today, and now that I have a 12-year-old daughter. I realize how wrong I was. Having a daughter has been the best thing I have ever done with my life. The amount of joy she brings into my life is indescribable.

So yes, you will be 60 years old, and yes, you will probably have an amazing life and a fantastic career.

You might have even discovered the cure for cancer. Yes, you may have a closet full of shoes and Gucci handbags.

But there are no family gatherings at Easter, Christmas, or Thanksgiving, you have no grandchildren laughing and playing in the backyard, and worst of all, you never will get to experience a son or a daughter looking you into your eyes and saying; "I love you, mommy."

Ask your grandparents, aunts, uncles, or parents what is really important to them. Sit down with them and ask them about their biggest regrets in life.

Nobody in their last years of life cares about their career. Nobody cares longer than 30 secs that you or your husband worked at Microsoft for 60 to 80 hours a week and that you designed the latest and the greatest newest user interface.

All they will ever care about is you, your husband, and your children.

It's called interdependence.

He needs you as much as you need him.

He has to face and overcome his fears about marrying you and trusting you, as much as you need to face and overcome your fears of trusting and marrying him.

The vast majority of men are good men, just like the vast majority of women are good women. And just like there are "bad" men in life, there are bad women.

Whether you are a man or a woman, when it comes to dating and relationships, my advice is always the same. You need to have and maintain high standards and boundaries, and **you really need to know this person intimately before agreeing to ever marry them.**

So, let's take a moment and talk about men's fears when it comes to marrying.

Because if you do not address these fears while dating, the chances of him ever asking you to marry him are very slim.

One day you will wake up. You will have been dating your man for four years, and try as you may, he won't propose, so you finally break up with him because you get so frustrated.

And then you get angry because you feel like you just wasted four years of your life.

But here's the problem. You never really knew him. You thought you did. But it turns out you didn't. **Because you always played it safe.** Because you never had the courage to be truly vulnerable with him and have deep, meaningful conversations about things that really mattered.

Because sooner or later, you are going to learn this very powerful lesson about men, dating, and relationships. **Playing it safe rarely gets you what you want.**

Playing it safe only gives players, users, abusers, and men too afraid to commit **a safe place to hide.**

You see, a lot of women complain about men committing, but most women never take the time to put themselves in a man's shoes and address their fears.

CHAPTER 26:
WHY MEN ARE AFRAID TO COMMIT.

INSIDE OUT DATING MAKEOVER

KEVIN BOYLE

It's not that men are afraid of commitment. It's that just like you, **men are afraid to commit to the WRONG person.**

Just like the wrong man can ruin your life, the wrong woman can ruin his.

Losing his freedom.

Losing access to variety.

Losing access to sex.

Losing 50% of everything he has if you should split up.

Losing access to children if you should split up.

Ending up married to a demanding, nagging wife.

Just as you are evaluating men while you are dating to see if he is the right one, men are evaluating you and your attitude towards men, marriage, dating, relationships, and most importantly, SEX!

If you ever want to move your relationship forward with your man, you need to understand his fears from his perspective and that he needs reassurance that you and him are on the same page when it comes to what you both want out of life.

And this requires deep, meaningful conversations.

So, what is the best way to communicate with a man?

From a place of true vulnerability.

Ladies, I know this sucks, and you are going to hate me for saying this, but you need to teach and model for men how to be vulnerable in your communication and your relationship with them.

We live in a culture where it has become ok to bash men and blame them for all of our relationship problems. And hear me out before you start throwing tomatoes and rotten vegetables at me.

In my inside-out transformational life coaching business with my clients, I have not had one woman ever tell me that she has been ever truly vulnerable with her man, not one woman who has said to me that she was willing to risk being open and vulnerable with her man and model for him what she says she wants from him.

My experience with women is that most women are really good at asking a lot of questions;

Where were you last night? How come you never call? When are we going to get married, or the infamous, how are you feeling?

But ladies, this is not communicating!

This is pushing and prodding, whining and complaining, issuing ultimatums, and for men, **this is annoying.**

Because to men, **this is not communicating.**

This is why men don't answer. This is why men walk away. This is why men have man caves.

And this is why men stall and why men do not commit.

Most women refuse or fail to have deep intimate conversations with their men because of their own wounds, their fears of rejection and hearing answers they don't want to hear, and their own need to do the work.

Their insecurities, the fear of confrontation, the fear of hearing the truth, and your fear of being truly vulnerable with your man, modeling, and saying what needs to be said;

"I know even thinking about ever getting married can be a huge scary thought. There are often times **when I ask myself, am I even ready for it?** And I don't know, but I do know that you are the love of my life. I am just curious, Scott, what are your biggest fears when it comes to even thinking about ever getting married?"

You cannot expect the world (read, your relationship, your man) to show up differently for you if you are not prepared to show up for it in the way that you say you want.

If you want your man to open up and be vulnerable with you. You need to open up and be vulnerable with him.

So, **what does being vulnerable look like?** Because when you first meet someone it is very easy to make the mistake of "over-sharing" and sending them running for the hills.

Telling someone you have just met about all of your medical problems, your mother's issues with mental illness, the fact that you have $110,000 in student loan debt, and that your last boyfriend who you dated for three years was abusive and toxic is a sure-fire way of ensuring that there will never be a second date.

How do you know what to share and what not to share?

One: Make sure that whatever you are about to share, that you have healed and let it go. That whatever it is, it no longer has a hold on you.

Two: share small pieces, share things that happened a long time ago, and just share enough to give your date an understanding of what happened.

Three: follow it up with a positive attitude. To show that you have grown and learned from the experience.

Four: Save the big stuff for when you have been dating for a while, and you have a history of sharing and being vulnerable with your partner.

How to have deeper, more meaningful conversations with men.

The second mistake most women make when it comes to having conversations with men is that they **wait until there is a problem**, and then they try to have these difficult conversations with men, but when you do; men feel attacked, they feel like they have been backed into a corner, they feel pressured, and then they withdraw, and you get exactly the opposite of what it is that you say you want.

So how do you have a meaningful conversation with a man without pushing him away?

It's through your willingness to be vulnerable, FIRST.

Which consists of three steps; gratitude, vulnerability, and intention.

And ladies, it's scary, I know, but wouldn't you like to know now rather than waste six months, 2, 3, 4 years, or more to only find out that you and your man are not compatible or on the same page when it comes to the important questions about life?

The 2nd Date: Finding out his attachment style.

IMPORTANT NOTE: The first date was about having fun, no agenda, no pressure, and seeing if the two of you have genuine chemistry and compatibility.

The second date is all about being able to answer one question, **is he willing, and is he able to have deep, meaningful conversations that matter?**

It is time to risk being vulnerable because **vulnerability is the key ANTIDOTE** to players, emotionally unavailable men, and men who are afraid to commit.

Step One: Gratitude.

You: "Wow, I am having such a great time. It's been a while since I have laughed this much!"

Gratitude is a compliment. Sincere, heartfelt, and genuine.

Gratitude is the single biggest reason that my wife and I are so happy together.

There is not a day that goes by that I don't thank my wife for something and that I don't tell her that she is the best thing that has ever happened to me.

Why? Because **gratitude comes from an abundance mindset**, it comes from a place of having instead of "getting," and let's be honest, when you are truly grateful for the life you have, for the people who are in it, it just naturally lights you up!

Step Two: Vulnerability

You: "I was talking to a good friend the other day, and we were talking about our lives and what it was like when we were growing up, and this is going to sound kind of silly, but I remember the first time my mom dropped me off at school, and I felt abandoned. I literally freaked out in front of the class, and I swear everyone thought I was nuts!"

Him: Oh wow, that sounds really horrible. What happened after that?

You: Actually, it turned out ok. I am a big believer that everything happens for a reason. I learned a very powerful lesson from that experience. I learned how to be ok with being alone.

NOTE: You MUST take your bad experience and turn it into a positive experience. **DO NOT dwell on the negative.**

Show your date that you have no attachment to it. Show him what you have learned from the experience or how you grew from it.

You: "Carl, have you ever felt like that? Abandoned or all alone?"

Give him lots of room and LISTEN.

How does he react?

Is he secure? He most likely will answer the question in a fairly balanced manner, sprinkling in the good with the bad. He will be open in his answers. He might even share with you that he has had some counseling.

Does he change the topic? You just shared something deeply intimate about yourself. How does he react?

The most important thing is not to focus on where you want the conversation to go. Leave it wide open as to where the conversation goes. Try to ask open-ended questions to explore even further.

Your main goal is to see how he responds to having deeper, more meaningful conversations that matter.

Is he avoidant? He may say he had a great childhood, but leave it at that with no specific stories to back it up.

He may shift his weight and look uncomfortable after you have asked the question. He may state that he has very little memory of his childhood in order to try and escape answering the question.

Is he anxious? He will generally be overly focused on the negative. He might even get pulled in to his anxiety about women, dating, and relationships and start relating his bad experiences to the present or his recent dating and relationship experiences.

Is he fearful? They most likely will get annoyed with your question. He might get defensive or try to dodge the question by giving you a short answer and then changing the topic.

Step Three: Intention

Now, this may not seem important, but it is just as CRITICALLY important as the other two steps. Your "intention" should be to show up with NO AGENDA, no end goal in mind, and no pre-determined answers.

Your intention should be to show up as being curious and understanding, as letting him know that you are a safe place for him to open up to, for him to now show you that he has also has a vulnerable side.

Make THAT your intention, and he will start to see you as a woman of value, a woman with a strong sense of self, a woman worthy of respect, a woman who is soft and warm because NO woman has ever communicated with him like this ever before.

Follow Up: With open-ended questions;

Start off with being vulnerable FIRST and sharing a bit of yourself.

You: "Sometimes I can be a little bit slow when it comes to trusting people."

Follow up with an open-ended question:

"I am just curious, how do you feel about getting close to people?" ("I am just curious" helps "soften" your communication.)

"Do you find it hard trusting people?"

"How does it affect you when you are out dating and wanting to have a relationship?"

Other topics you should take the time to explore on future dates are:

- What are his hopes and dreams?
- Is he a planner with goals? Like how many children and a family?
- Is he competent when it comes to money, debt, and finances?
- Marriage roles and sharing housework.
- Handling difficult conversations and conflict.

Notes: do not try to "cram" all of these conversations into one or two dates.

Try to space out these conversations. Have some fun dates in between dates where you are having deeper, more meaningful conversations, and most importantly, go with the flow!

The boyfriend, girlfriend conversation. (Whenever you feel ready.)

You need to trust your gut on this. When you think about having a boyfriend-girlfriend conversation with him. How do you feel deep down inside? Is it with butterflies of excitement or butterflies of impending doom?

If you are feeling anxious, I suggest you grab a separate piece of paper and go to page 140 and actually put pen to paper and answer the questions separately and see if you might be over-investing into someone who in your heart of hearts you know might not be the best match for you.

Gratitude:

You: "These last few weeks/months have been incredible, I feel so comfortable with you, and I am having so much fun!"

Vulnerability:

You: I feel a little bit awkward right now, and if I am being completely honest, a little bit vulnerable because I can see myself falling for you and wanting to take this to the next level.

Now that we have had a chance to spend some time together, do you want us to be boyfriend/girlfriend?

If he says no, in any way, shape, or form. It's OVER. You are NOT THE ONE.

It's time to pack up and move on.

Note: Now I know someone is going to ask. Well, don't you want to know why? No, I don't. The fastest, and easiest way to get anyone to decide on what is important to them, is to take it away from them. As hard as it is, you must always be willing to walk away from the negotiating table.

Remember: Hire slow, fire FAST!

Intention:

If he says yes.

You: Awesome! So, can we establish some ground rules moving forward where we can agree on what that will look like?

Lean in, get soft… "So tell me, what makes an amazing girlfriend to you?"

Ok, we can do that!

You: "For me, I want to know that you and I are exclusive, that you are not on any dating apps, and that you are not chasing any other girls or having sex with other girls."

You: "I want to know it is just you and me. Deal?"

The next date;

After the boyfriend, girlfriend conversation date – NO serious topics. Focus purely on fun and having a good time!

Now I know you do not want to do this. I know every single fiber of your being is saying, Kevin, I cannot do this, I cannot be this vulnerable with someone.

But do you want to know what one of the single biggest problems I have when coaching women who come to me with relationship problems?

They have been dating the same man for four, six, or twelve years thinking they have been building something and that one day it will lead to marriage.

And then it happens one day the man just gets up and leaves, or you find out he has huge financial problems, he does or doesn't want kids, or he is just coasting along in the relationship, never willing to commit, because he is hiding. Hiding from his fears, hiding from his fear of being truly seen.

If you cannot or will not take the time to have vulnerable conversations with men, and if you are unwilling to model them first to ensure that deep, meaningful conversations happen, **it carries a HUGE risk.**

Because think about it this way. It takes on average two years to meet someone, then you have two to three years to get to know them.

Then if all of the stars are in alignment and you are both on the same page, it takes another one to two years to plan a wedding.

Mr. Wrong can potentially waste four to seven years of your LIFE, if not longer!

The "Talk." How to move your relationship closer to marriage and get him to talk about commitment without scaring the hell out of him.

Gratitude:

You: "Carl, you (**insert,** genuine heartfelt compliment)."

Vulnerability:

You: "I was talking to my dad the other day. I was talking to him about how even **just thinking** about ever being married scares the heck out of me."

You: "I think for me, my deepest fear is opening myself up to relying on someone else."

You: "I am just curious, Carl, when it comes to **even thinking** about ever being married, **what is your biggest fear?"**

LISTEN.

Ask OPEN ended questions.

Ask why. "And why do you think that might happen?"

Intention:

Lean in, get soft… "So, tell me, when you think about what it would be like to have an incredibly loving, sexy wife. What do you think of, what does your dream wife look like to you?"

You: "Oh, I can do so much better than that!"

You: "I have a secret I want to share with you. I want to always be your girlfriend. In fact, I want to apply for permanent wife status!"

Vulnerable meaningful conversations are the best ANTIDOTE to men who are not ready and who may never be ready. He may be a great guy, but if you want to have a family, do you really want to take the risk of not knowing where his head and his heart are?

Vulnerable, meaningful conversations are an opportunity to deepen your bonds, connection, and commitment to each other and add to the health of your relationship.

The other problem I find with a lot of women who are dating and trying to find the one is that they like to "rush" these conversations.

They want the answers right now, and they do not want to waste any time!

So, trust me when I say this. No man wants to waste his time or money on you either. As much as you say you are looking for the "right" one, so is he.

But just like you don't like a man with an agenda of "him wanting to use you for sex on the first, second, or third date. He does not want to date a woman with an agenda either. He does not want to date a woman who, through her energy, words, or questions, is pushing for commitment before she even knows a guy.

Your radar is on the lookout for men who are only dating for sex. His radar is on the lookout for women whose "clocks are ticking" and who are on the hunt for commitment.

So, do not rush these conversations by having them on the first date, because you and I both know men can be very fast runners :p

CHAPTER 27:
NEVER STOP BEING HIS GIRLFRIEND.

INSIDE OUT DATING MAKEOVER

KEVIN BOYLE

This is probably the most politically incorrect thing I have said in this entire book, and I know I have said many, but here it goes…

Most men do not want a "wife."

That is a social construct that he must conform to if he wants to be with you.

Every man wants you to never stop being cool, never stop being easy to be with, and NEVER stop being his GIRLFRIEND.

Because the reality is, girlfriends, don't nag. Wives do.

Yes, a man will "wife you up," but that's because he wants you to be his permanent girlfriend.

Remember, the real challenge for a man is getting the girl, and the real challenge for a woman is getting him to commit.

So, be the woman he wants to commit to!

Be his permanent girlfriend, give him some peace, risk being vulnerable, risk looking or trying to be sexy once in a while, risk looking awkward and a little bit dorky. Trust me, he's not going to care.

Men do not think the same way you do. Stop overanalyzing, being so self-conscious, and nit-picking yourself apart.

STOP trying to be so perfect all of the time. Men would prefer that you be a little bit imperfect because that would then give us permission to be a little bit imperfect as well!

Because when you are too focused on always being perfect, you are NOT giving yourself enough permission to be PLAYFUL.

If a man is with you, it's because he accepts and loves all of you. He accepts and loves the hip dips, the cellulite, the big red pimple on your nose, and the big arms, all of it!

Never stop flirting, being playful, and letting him know that he is your big burly manly man!

LEAN into him, I mean really physically lean into him. Let him feel your torso press up to his. Put your arms around him, press yourself into him and kiss him.

And say, "I used to be so sweet and innocent before I met you: p."

Or you could playfully push him away and say;

You: "You need to stop."

You: Whisper in his ear. "Being such a bad boy!"

Some tips on how to let your man be your "hero."

- Try to figure out a way to support him in his goals. Help bring out the best in your man. You two are a team. Remember, a man is at his best when he feels that he is doing something meaningful and being something meaningful.

- Open up and be vulnerable with him. Show him that you do trust him.

- Text him; "Just a little message to let you know that you are my hero, and I am so happy to have you in my life!"

- Ask for his advice about something, and then say, "You know that sounds like a great idea. I am going to try that!"

- Compliment him when he least expects it. "You know, honey, you really do a lot for me, and I appreciate it."

- Praise him and **help make him look good** out in public in front of his boss, his friends, your friends, and both your families.

- Conversely, do NOT dimmish him in public.

- Give him a honey to-do list, post it where he can see it, and then leave it. Don't nag him, don't bother him about it, just let him do it. And if he forgets to do it, find a way to highlight it for the next day so he can't miss it. Have fun with it!

- Leave "manly" things on your honey to-do list for him to do, and then enthusiastically thank him and reward him for doing things for you.

Trust me, if you do this right, he will be looking for things to do for you!

- When he wants to help you, let him!

- Let him know when he does something that you really like or when he does something that makes you happy.

- NEVER stop being his girlfriend, and trust me on this, he will devote his life to you!

No man who marries you and has a family with you expects you to be his girlfriend all of the time. All we ask is that you do not forget about that part of yourself.

CHAPTER 28:
LIFE ONLY GIVES YOU MORE OF WHO YOU ARE BEING. DATING WITH AN ABUNDANCE MINDSET.

INSIDE OUT DATING MAKEOVER

KEVIN BOYLE

"Don't get anyone pregnant, and for God's sake, always make sure you are wearing a condom."

That was my dad's well-intentioned all-encompassing best advice regarding girls, dating, and sex.

And you guessed it. I am pretty sure the first time I had sex, I wasn't wearing a condom. It was New Year's Eve. I was seventeen years old, and my mom hated my girlfriend (she thought my girlfriend was one of those "bad" girls).

To be completely honest, I had no intention of losing my virginity that night. It just kind of happened.

I was drunk, she led me upstairs, took my clothes off, and that's all I remember.

I am not sharing that story with you for any reason other than to get you to ask one very important question.

Why would my girlfriend want to have sex with me?

It couldn't have been that much fun. I never asked for it, we hadn't talked about it, and truth be told, I did not feel ready for it.

I can only guess. Perhaps she needed to feel close to someone. Perhaps something was missing in her life. I know her dad was pretty strict. Maybe she thought it would make me like her more. I'll never know. It's not like at 17, I was that great of a conversationalist or particularly bright.

But I do know this.

I was very lonely as a teenager, and maybe she was too.

Have you ever wondered why sometimes we can be alone and never feel lonely, while at other times we can be surrounded by our friends and family or in a relationship and still feel "lonely"?

Well, now, many years later, I finally understand why.

It essentially comes down to three things;

- Our beliefs about how we see ourselves in relation to others.
- How connected we feel to ourselves through self-love and self-acceptance.
- And how engaged we are in the life that we are currently living.

These three things affect how we show up for ourselves when we are dating and when we are in a relationship, and it also affects how we experience others and how they experience us.

For as long as I can remember, I have always had this belief that I was not good enough. As a teenager, I was skinny, and I was very self-conscious about being skinny, and it didn't help that my dad made me feel even more self-conscious about being skinny.

As we start to self-judge, this belief becomes a wall that we carry around with us. And in this constant judgment, it separates us from others. We start to see others as either more than us, or we see ourselves as less than. Because who could possibly ever love someone as skinny, as "flawed," imperfect, or as awkward as me?

We carry this belief, into every social interaction, onto every date, and into every relationship. We show up as needy, guarded, self-conscious, and wanting to prove that we are worthy of love and acceptance.

And because we show up as self-conscious and needy, we repel others, further reinforcing our feeling that we are not enough and that there is something "wrong" with us.

Or we overcorrect.

I will protect myself before anyone can ever hurt me. I will be aloof. I will be guarded and untrusting. I will put up an invisible wall, so no one can ever hurt me.

In either case, we never experience a genuinely heartfelt, real connection with anyone.

So, what do most people do? They turn to sex. Because if we are unable to connect with people emotionally, for whatever reason, and there are a lot, trust me, sex becomes one of the few ways many of us know how to experience and how to get the intimacy our soul longs for.

And that's why our divorce rate in our society is so high and even higher in second and third marriages.

We do not have a good relationship with ourselves.

We do not fully accept and love ourselves.

And we do not know how to experience true emotional intimacy with others because it scares the crap out of us.

This leads to the single biggest reason why I believe you are probably still single and why you have not found the love of your life.

And before we get to it, I want to share with you one of my favorite quotes of all time from "A Return to Love" by Marianne Williamson.

"Our greatest fear is not that we are inadequate. Our greatest fear is that we are powerful beyond measure. It is our light, not our darkness that most frightens us. We ask ourselves, who am I to be brilliant, fabulous, gorgeous, talented? Actually, who are you not to be? You are a child of God. You're playing small, doesn't serve the world."

And that's what I have done for most of my life. Played small.

So, let me ask you a question.

When you first meet someone, when are they at their most attractive?

Is it really about looks? Yes, looks are important, but you and I know, looks only keep you interested in a person for what, maybe the first 5 or 10 minutes?

What is it that really draws us to a person and makes you think, I want to be with that person?

To me, a person is at their most attractive when they are living their life with passion, when they are out living their life and enjoying themselves.

To me, a person is at their most attractive when they truly love and accept themselves. Because when a person truly loves and accepts themselves, there is a calmness about them, there is a quiet strength and confidence about them. You know what their boundaries are, and you respect those boundaries simply because they are so grounded in who they are at the moment because they no longer have the need to prove themselves worthy to anyone.

And finally, to me, a person is at their most attractive when they live their life as though they don't need me. They don't need me to help validate how worthy they feel about themselves, and they don't need me to help fill up any emptiness that may be inside of them.

That's when a person is the most attractive to me. When you become that which is what you say you want in another person, that is when you will start to attract men from the very best version of yourself, instead of from a place of insecurity, fear, loneliness, emptiness, desperation, woundedness or damage.

You will finally start living your life from a place of having, instead of from a place of trying "to get."

Most men and women imagine the partner of their dreams as being larger than life and having an interesting, adventurous life that they want to be part of and share.

Whatever your parents or caregivers did not give you, whatever you feel is missing deep down inside of you, the answer is always the same.

Self-acceptance, self-love, and getting out and living a fully engaged life.

When you are truly living the life that makes you happy, and you are happy with who you are in that life, you will never have to look to a man to fill that void.

And when you stop looking to men to fill that emptiness deep down inside of you, your relationships with men will change because their experience of you will change.

This leads to this one inescapable truth about men, dating, and relationships.

Men are irresistibly attracted to a woman who lives her life as though she does not need them.

But the "does not need him" doesn't come from a place of aloofness, a place of guardedness, a place of disdain or judgment.

It comes from a place of a "chill" vibe towards men. You like them, but you don't "need" them.

You don't "need" men because you have an ABUNDANCE mindset!

An abundance mindset means that I am grounded in that I LOVE who I am, I LOVE who I am being, and I LOVE my life.

When you have an abundance mindset, it shifts your energy when you are dating. No longer do you approach dating from a place of scarcity.

When we date from a place of scarcity, our experience of dating is like a roller coaster ride, with extreme highs and extreme lows.

When we first meet someone, we get so excited that we start filling up the days and future planning. We get lost in our own heads without really even knowing someone.

And when it doesn't work out? We get sad. We get disappointed.

Because if we are being 100% honest with ourselves, we are living a life of scarcity. We put so much into this date. We invest so much of ourselves into this one person, and more often than not, we create this "fantasy" relationship with someone we barely know.

If you want to experience success in your dating life, you must have an abundance mindset.

I LOVE who I am, I LOVE who I am being, and I LOVE my life.

This is the kind of woman he will be irresistibly drawn to. This is the kind of woman he will bring his "A" game to. This is the kind of woman he will commit himself to win over because he knows, anything less, he risks losing her or never getting a chance in the first place.

And you have to remember this, this is a game he wants to WIN.

Remember earlier, I had mentioned that life rarely gives you what you want. It's not how the universal law of attraction works.

Life only gives you more **of who you are being.**

So instead of being lonely, instead of feeling or being "empty," instead of feeling or being guarded and untrusting.

Why not be what you say you want?

Why not be more loving?

This is the one dramatic SHIFT in your mindset that will bring you everything in life you have ever wanted.

If life only gives you more of who you are being, then why not be more loving towards who you are and who you are being?

Love yourself fully and unconditionally by finally healing your wounds from the past and healing and letting go of any disempowering limiting beliefs you might have about yourself, like, "I am not good enough."

Love your life by becoming more engaged in it, and start living your best life now, regardless of whether you have a man to share it with or not.

And when do you make these two powerful shifts in your life?

You will become absolutely irresistible.

You will be living a life of abundance.

This is the real journey; this is how you find your true soulmate.

For you to provide for yourself that which you previously looked for in others.

There is no more powerful validation than the validation you have for yourself.

There is no more powerful love than the love that you have for yourself.

Imagine for a moment being the most powerful, confident, joyful, loving version of yourself?

How would your life be different? If you no longer cared what other people thought because you had supreme confidence that everything about you is enough, that you are enough, that your life is enough?

Imagine waking up every day and feeling like you are the most beautiful woman in the world.

Imagine walking into a room and being this incredibly beautiful glowing light that attracts men and women, where men approach you, and you feel sexy and confident, you feel grounded, and you feel at ease in your own skin.

Imagine being attracted to a whole new level of man. A man who doesn't play games and who's eager to share his life with you and ready to commit to you.

Imagine being able to spot red flags right away and being confident enough in yourself to trust your gut and walk away instead of staying too long because you feel lonely or afraid that you might not ever find anyone else again.

Imagine only spending time with quality men who have long-term potential, allowing you to find Mr. Right so much faster.

If you want to see massive results in your dating and romantic life, it's through self-love, self-acceptance, and self-validation. When you change the way you see the world from the "inside," it will change the way you show up for men on the outside.

It's ironic when you think about it. We all have a fundamental understanding that no one is "perfect." We certainly accept our friends and family members as less than "perfect." Still, generally, we are unable to accept even the smallest flaws, imperfections, or mistakes in ourselves.

If you ever have wanted to feel more grounded and more confident in your life, it's through self-acceptance. That is the challenge of self-love, self-acceptance, and becoming our own perfect soulmate. Going inside and looking for the parts of ourselves that we find distasteful or the parts that we don't like is the path to feeling more grounded and confident.

We know it's something we shouldn't do, but we carry so much shame with us. The shame of the mistakes we have made, shame in the judgments that we carry about ourselves from our peers, and shame about our judgments of others. We label the parts of ourselves that we don't like as "bad" and secretly loathe ourselves for it.

It's certainly how I used to live my life, looking for the next relationship to save me, save me from the fact that if I was being completely honest, I did not love the life I was living. I was coasting, hoping that one day I would finally meet the person who would give me the love I couldn't or wouldn't give myself.

The reason we experience loneliness and emptiness in our lives is that we are constantly looking for love "out there."

Most of us live a life of distraction. We look for connection and for validation "out there," and we become disconnected from ourselves.

We live in the past or the future. A past filled with regret or shame and a future of "hope and prayers," that one day our lives will be different.

But your life is right now. It is in this present moment.

Now is the time to become your own best friend, commit to doing your personal growth work, and live a life of abundance. And as you "show up" for yourself, the loneliness will start to disappear, and you will make this huge wonderful shift into BEING the most powerful, loving version of yourself.

And when you start living a life that is fully engaged and self-accepting, you will fall in love with yourself.

So, the question becomes, what steps can you take to start living your life as fully engaged and fully self-accepting?

There are two steps.

One: We need to heal the wounds of our past, we need to heal and let go of our disempowering limiting beliefs and our own unhealthy relationship patterns, and we need to stop letting our fears and our insecurities hold us back from living our best lives ever!

Because no matter how engaged we become in our lives, if we still have this "messiness" living deep down inside of us, we will still keep bringing this part of ourselves into every social interaction, every date, and every relationship.

I cannot stress this enough, the biggest mistake I made was thinking that time heals all wounds. But what I learned is this, no, life does not work that way.

There are some wounds that time does not heal, and if there is a part of you that is damaged or wounded, even if you do meet a "good" guy, there is a very good chance that you may either self-sabotage or push him away.

Two: We need to go out and start living our lives in the "real world," expand our social circle, and do things that allow us to meet new people and bring us joy!

I'll be honest, there were times in my life when I was my own worst enemy. There were times when I lived a life of isolation and distraction. I turned to dating apps because they were so easy, and if I am being 100% honest, I got lazy.

Dating apps and social media give the illusion of choice that there is this vast number of people to pick from, and it helped me feel like I was doing something to meet people, but they were actually a big reason why I had grown so disillusioned with dating, and why I had stopped trusting women.

When working with clients, one of my favorite exercises to help them get back into being more engaged with their life and living a life of abundance is to ask them to do a simple exercise whereby they ask and answer four questions;

What ACTIVITY or hobby can I do that will get me out of the house, where I can learn a new skill, improve upon one or engage with groups of people?

For example, you could; join a church group, a business networking group, art gallery opening, wine tastings, take a night class, attend book readings, or one of my favorites, join meetup.com

What PHYSICAL activity can I do that will get me out of the house, engaging with groups of people, where I can learn a new skill or improve upon one that I already know?

For example, you could; play softball, or volleyball, take a spin class, take up dancing, or join a running club.

What cause can I VOLUNTEER my time and energy towards that will help the planet, help people, help my community that will get me out of the house, engaging with groups of people, where I can learn a new skill or improve upon one that I already know?

Dog rescue, cancer, working with youth, attending community and charity events, etc.

This will give you three activities a week where you are getting yourself out of the house and more engaged with your life.

Be open to possibilities! Meet new people and start conversations. If you show up as loving, warm, and kind. You will start to get invites to parties, to events where you will have even more opportunities to even meet more people!

Because there is another benefit to being more social and getting out more and meeting more people.

The biggest problem you are going to encounter with dating is lying. And that is only one antidote, only one way to protect yourself. Stop dating men you don't know.

Get off social media, get off dating apps and go out, live your life and meet men in person!

The fourth exercise in becoming more engaged in our lives is to take the time to answer life's **BIG** question.

What is the meaning of life?

What I have found is that the answer to "What is the meaning of life" is actually a better question, "What would give my life more meaning?"

When I framed the question this way, it was like the clouds lifted, and the answer came immediately to me.

It's helping others.

This is what I want my legacy to be. This is how I want to be remembered by my friends, family, loved ones, and society.

Helping others has become the main "theme" of my life. It underlies the reason for everything that I do.

The question then becomes how can I be more specific in how I plan on living out this legacy and how can I "help and be of service to others?"

My mission statement:

My fondest childhood memories are family get-togethers and dinners during holidays, Thanksgiving, and Sunday nights.

I wrote this book because I believe in the value of family and I want to help bring men and women back together again.

By EMPOWERING our daughters and women of all ages to live their best lives ever by helping them become the most POWERFUL, confident, joyful, loving version of themselves to better understand men and why men do what they do so women of today can finally attract, meet, and keep the most amazing man of their dreams!

I do this by helping women get to the root causes of why their relationships are not working out, by helping them heal their wounds of their past, heal and let go of any disempowering limiting beliefs and unhealthy relationship patterns that they might have so they can finally get out of their own way of having the kind of life and relationships that they say that they have always wanted!

So why not make your mission statement (for now) to be 'the' person who helps bring singles together who are looking for serious relationships by hosting a potluck dinner every 2nd or 4th week?

Start a Meetup for singles called **"Potluck for Singles"** and ask everyone to bring a dish and make it a dinner party! After dinner, you can host a poker night.

What man can resist delicious food and being able to spend the night with a bunch of beautiful single women playing poker?

And the best part? Once you have your group of regulars, and as you build up your community of friends, you can start actively planning day trips for hiking, movie nights, going out to comedy clubs and special events, etc.!

Trust me if you do these four exercises consistently and if you finally heal and let go of your wounds from the past so that you are living your life as the most powerful, confident, joyful, loving version of yourself.

You will start living a life FULL of ABUNDANCE.

And when you start living your life with an abundance mindset. You will experience a powerful and amazing inside-out, life-changing TRANSFORMATION.

And when you do? Know that that love and the most AMAZING man of your dreams will be waiting for you just around the corner!

BONUS CHAPTER:
THE ONE CRITICALLY IMPORTANT LIFE LESSON THAT EVERYONE NEEDS TO KNOW.

INSIDE OUT DATING MAKEOVER

KEVIN BOYLE

As a father, if you were to ask me what is the single most valuable life lesson that I would like to pass down to my daughter it would be this.

"The universe has a wisdom of its own, and unfortunately, it rarely will give you what you want.

It only gives you **MORE OF WHO YOU ARE BEING.**"

If you want something different, you have to accept that whatever you are doing right now is probably not working or else you would already have it!

Whatever you want in life, you have to grow into it. You have to work for it, and you have to be willing to continually challenge your beliefs, your attitude, and your behaviors.

I have had several readers reach out to me to ask me to go into more detail about **what is the "work,"** and what steps they can take in their own personal growth work to help them become the very best version of themselves and to finally leave their painful wounds of their past, in the past where they belong.

The cold hard truth is that for the vast majority of us, **we are the ones that are getting in our way** of having and living the kind of life that we say we want and it's because of our internal landscape.

So, I have one question for you.

Who do you want to be?

Because if you want to be happy in your life, you don't find it – you create it.

If you want to be successful in your job or career, you don't find it, you create it.

If you want to be happy and fulfilled in your relationships, you don't find that perfect person – the perfect person does not exist – you create it every single day in the person who YOU are being.

It's not very fun when you finally come to the sobering realization that we are all ultimately responsible for our own behavior, our own unhealthy relationship patterns and who we choose to be attracted to, who we attract, and most importantly who we choose to stay in a relationship with.

In hindsight, my last relationship before my wife, the painful breakup that ensued, and her leaving me was probably the greatest gift she could have ever given me in my own personal development.

It forced me to face my own personal demons. It forced me to take a good hard look at the type of woman I was attracted to and the type that I was attracting.

It forced me to finally do the work and to heal my painful wounds from my past, my unhealthy relationship and dating attachment patterns and behaviors, and to heal and let go of my disempowering limiting beliefs, that I was carrying around within me that "I was not good enough."

I had come to the point in my life where I had come to the painful realization that if you are still using the same bait. Read if you are dating damaged in some way, if you have lost faith in the opposite sex and you no longer trust them, or if you are still carrying around old wounds with you. You will only end up bleeding all over people who have most likely never hurt you.

And you will only catch more of the same kind of fish.

I have a question for you. Because this is the question, I found myself asking myself after that very painful breakup.

When you are 60 years old, **wouldn't it be nice to look back on your life and know that you had an amazing life** with an amazing partner who really loved and cherished you and who had your back. Someone you could count on to be there for you when things got tough because we all know how hard life can be?

I know that's what I wanted, and that's when I knew if I ever wanted that, that I had to do the work.

So, how do you know you need to do the work?

Have you ever caught yourself saying there are no good men left? That all men are cheaters, all men are users, that all men are afraid of commitment, all men are jerks, all men want is sex, that I am just not good enough, that I am probably going to die alone, etc…

The reality is, that not all men are cheaters, not all men are jerks, not all men are users, and not all men are afraid to commit.

This is going to hurt when I say this.

This is your belief system and your experiences with men. **The one constant in all of this, is you.**

With all of the Dr. Phil's, the relationship and dating gurus, the thousands of self-help books, life coaches, the Tony Robbins, Oprah Winfrey's, and thousands upon thousands of YouTube videos on how to make your relationships better, the divorce rate is going up, not down!

Clearly, what we are doing is NOT WORKING.

We are not getting to the core reasons for all of the dysfunction in modern-day relationships, and why people are so unhappy.

We need to be honest with ourselves about our own deeply held disempowering limiting beliefs when it comes to how we feel about ourselves and our lives, and our very unhealthy relationship and dating attachment patterns and behaviors.

For example, as a child, I looked up to my father.

I will admit, I put him on a pedestal. He could do no wrong. The problem was he was very critical. And once his words that I wasn't good enough, that I could not do anything right, that I was not deserving were in my subconscious mind, it was recorded like a record player for the rest of my life.

My subconscious mind played you are not deserving, you are not enough, you are stupid over and over again, and that's what life gave me.

Because of this, I felt so much shame growing up, and I would recreate that shame over and over again in dating, in my relationships, and in my life.

Because of this belief that I was not good enough, **I would often overcompensate in relationships** by trying to prove that I was worthy, and that's how I became a people pleaser.

I remember old girlfriends telling me that I was trying too hard, and through this dynamic, I would experience even more shame.

On top of all of that, **I also had this intense fear of abandonment.** Can you imagine self-sabotaging relationships through my people-pleasing behavior and also having an intense fear of abandonment? It was chaos! Because both fears fed into each other.

I became needy and messy, and **needy and messy is not an attractive quality in a person.**

Shame, people-pleasing, disempowering limiting beliefs, these unhealthy relationship patterns and behaviors. Followed me from relationship to relationship. They became part of who I was being, and they **ruined all of my relationships.**

This is not about whether you are a good person or not or whether you are trying hard enough or not. Try and try as we might, we simply cannot escape the painful wounds of our past, our own disempowering limiting beliefs, and the pains of our own self-judgment.

I allowed myself to be disempowered by my father because I didn't know any better, but as an adult, I was now disempowering myself by not healing and letting go of it.

I had convinced myself that I was powerless to create the kind of life that I wanted because, deep down, I did not feel like who I was being was good enough for it, that I didn't feel like I deserved it, and that, ultimately, I was not worthy of it.

Because when you have low self-esteem, or you have this belief deep inside of you that you are not good enough, you are going to look for and attract a relationship partner who agrees with how you see yourself.

And this is where we need to talk about relationship and dating attachment styles and how they affect our ability to form deep loving relationships and ultimately how we communicate with the opposite sex and resolve conflict.

Essentially, the experiences we have as children with our primary caregivers will have a lasting effect on the characteristics we display as adults and how we show up in our romantic, relationship, and dating lives.

Earlier I had given two examples of how I experienced lack of emotional safety and security in my life at a very early age; one, when my mom dropped me off for the very first time at school – I felt abandoned for the first time in my life. And with my father. How he was quite abusive, very critical and judgmental in his nature which led to my belief that I was not good enough and where I felt like I had to continually prove myself as worthy in relationships.

Because of these vulnerabilities I experienced as a child, I struggled throughout most of my adult life with being vulnerable with others, with trusting others, and with connecting and communicating in relationships.

I was unaware that my thinking, feeling, and belief patterns were around my attachment style and was the root cause of my subconscious desire to avoid becoming too close to other people because I did not want to feel rejected or abandoned ever again.

Attachment styles can be broken down into **four primary categories:**

1. Secure
2. Avoidant
3. Anxious
4. Fearful-Avoidant

Before getting into the different types of attachment styles, I think it's important to note, that people can have varying degrees under different circumstances of different attachment styles.

For instance, someone who has been in a relationship for a long time might over that time become more secure in the relationship and still have anxious patterns while exhibiting more characteristics of a secure person.

While another person may have a completely opposite experience in their adult relationship where there is a lot of chaos and conflict.

Also, attachment style is very fluid, someone may be secure most of the time in relationship, but during stress, arguments or disagreements with their significant other they may become triggered into avoidant, anxious, or fearful thoughts and behaviors.

So rather than look at all of the different attachment styles first, I thought it would be interesting to start with the secure attachment style, and if you are a parent or you want to be one in the future. How do we raise our children so they feel more grounded and more secure in their relationships with us and with others?

First of all, since children take their cues from us, we need to be completely honest with ourselves in how we are showing up in our own relationship, how we communicate, and how we handle conflict in our relationships.

We need to heal and let go of our own triggers, our own wounds, our own unhealthy relationship patterns and behaviors and our own disempowering limiting beliefs.

And it is critically important to keep in mind that there is no such thing as an ideal parent.

Keeping that in mind, if you want to bring up a child who has a secure attachment style, there are five essential conditions that you, as a parent, need to take into consideration.

1. Your child has a sense of security

If your child has the sense that they are being safeguarded and protected, they will feel not only physically safe, but at this age it is actually more important that they feel and experience emotional safety and security.

A caregiver who is sensitive to their child's needs can be fiercely protective without being overbearing, intrusive, or dismissive. Allowing for your child's independence and space necessary to discover their world, with a watchful eye from you.

2. Your child has the experience of feeling like they are seen and heard.

Parents that are attuned to their children are able to effectively interpret their children's cues and respond appropriately to their requirements.

Children can learn about the consequences of their actions through reactions that are attuned to their needs.

As a young child when we set up expectations with Chiara, we would often ask her – if this doesn't happen what do you think would be a fair consequence?

And often times she would come up with consequences that were actually greater than what I was initially thinking. Allowing me to walk it back and give her a win, allowing my daughter to experience compromising in a relationship.

The end outcome for the child is that they develop a sense of mastery over their lives from an early age on and that they also can depend on people who are important to them to negotiate with them and to work out a fair compromise.

They learn at an early age, that they can express their needs and that those needs will be met by people who they care about and who care about them.

3. Your child experiences feelings of consolation, calming, and reassurance.

When children are upset or distressed, his or her caregivers should reassure and comfort the child so that the youngster can return to an emotionally stable state.

The child will be better able to establish an internal model of being soothed and comforted if you assist them in learning how to handle their anguish and frustrations.

Your child will eventually acquire the capacity to regulate his or her own anguish and to self-soothe as time passes.

My own personal feeling is that expressing emotions, like crying is actually quite healthy for a child or as an adult. I have always let my daughter know that she can cry in front of me, and that there is no judgement.

As long as the crying is not a manipulation, but an expression of distress or a need to release emotions I've told Chiara she should not feel ashamed if she feels a need to cry.

4. Your child feels appreciated

The experience of being appreciated serves as the basis for the development of positive self-esteem.

Parents who are successful in fostering strong self-esteem in their children consistently focus on the positive aspects of their children's values, beliefs, and accomplishments.

I have always promoted very positive words of encouragement with my daughter through stories about how to handle gossip for example.

To that end I am always letting my daughter know that I think she is a good person, that I am proud of her accomplishments, winning the leadership and service awards at her school (note you have to be specific about what these are, so your child feels seen and recognized) and that often times when people gossip about you it's because they are wounded in some way, it's a mirror of the pain that is inside of them and more often than not it has nothing to do with her. To stay away from that person and continue to be a good person.

And you know what, her self esteem is so high, she's so smart – and she gets it. She gets the emotional support, security and safety that she needs at her age from us and she's able to learn and grow as a person.

5. Your child is encouraged to be curious and investigate their environment.

Lastly, children need to have the sense that they are supported without judgement in order to explore their world. As a parent I always encourage my daughter to face her fears and I will tell her stories to remind her on how she has overcome her fear of learning how to swim, learning how to ride a bike and then take that learning and encourage her to try new things, to encourage her to aspire to be whatever she wants to be in life knowing that I am there to catch her, if she should fall to help her develop autonomy and independence.

This feeling of safety enables your child to venture out into the world, make discoveries, achieve their goals, and learn from their mistakes. It is through these experiences that your child will cultivate a healthy, independent, powerful, and one-of-a-kind sense of self.

And the best part of this type of parenting style? Is that there is no need for you to worry about being perfect all of the time – because that's another discussion you can have with your children. That no one, their teachers, their parents, gov't leaders are perfect, we all have flaws and quirks – but what is important is do we treat others with kindness and respect?

Over time you will learn that you're parenting or relationship with your child becomes secure because of your child's trust in you and their love for you.

The Avoidant Attachment Style.

A child may develop an avoidant attachment if their primary caregiver does not demonstrate enough concern or responsiveness to the child beyond the provision of basic necessities such as food and shelter.

This forces the child as a means of coping to put their own problems and requirements out of their mind in order to keep the peace and remain in close proximity to their caregiver.

They continue to struggle and experience negative emotions such as anxiety, disappointment, confusion, or despair, but they do so alone at the cost of having to minimize the significance of such emotions.

Around thirty percent of persons in today's society exhibit patterns of avoidant attachment.

Signs That You Have an Avoidant Attachment Relationship and Dating Style.

As they get older, children that have an avoidant attachment style may show symptoms of it in later on in their relationship and dating style;

- They struggle to express their feelings and thoughts about important matters

- They experience unease and discomfort in situations involving close physical proximity and touch
- They may accuse their partner of being extremely jealous or possessive to an unhealthy degree
- They often refuse to accept assistance or emotional support from other people
- They have often had an intense fear of intimacy, and as a relationship grows stronger over time, they may actually ghost their partner or sabotage the relationship in some way.
- They have a strong need to express personal independence and freedom to the detriment of their romantic relationships.
- During times of stress, not looking to their partners for emotional support – or conversely being unavailable to their partner for support.

The Anxious Attachment Style.

Anxious attachment is almost always the result of parenting that is both inattentive and or inconsistent.

Low self-esteem, an intense dread of being rejected or abandoned, an "emotional hunger" to be in a relationship, fear of being alone, and an overly possessive or jealous nature in romantic relationships are all characteristics of this attachment style.

This type of attachment is generally characterized by a child's inability to securely attach to their caregivers emotionally usually because of their caregiver's inability to emotionally bond with their children, intrusiveness in the child's life by the caregiver, some type of abuse, or it can also be possible that the caregivers are too overbearing or overprotective. It's possible that they're using their child to satisfy their own "hunger" for emotion safety and security or to portray themselves in a specific light to the outside world (for example, as the perfect parent).

Signs That You Have an Anxious Attachment Relationship and Dating Style.

- You over function in relationships
- You become a people pleaser in relationships
- You worry and obsess over whether or not you will ever meet "the one"
- You think you can't ever be happy unless you are in a relationship with someone
- Struggle with self-confidence or low self-esteem
- Do not feel worthy of love
- Need constant reassurance that they or the relationship is "ok"
- They are not comfortable with being alone for extended periods.

The Fear/Avoidant Attachment Style.

The fearful avoidant attachment style is the most challenging among the insecure attachment styles because it involves both avoidant and anxious behaviors in dating and relationships. Children who have been verbally, physically, or sexually abused or assaulted are frequently found to have this attachment style.

When a child's caregivers, who should be their first and foremost source of safety, instead become a cause of intense anxiety for the child, an attachment style known as fearful-avoidant develops.

That was me. And in adulthood, people who have this attachment style behave in a highly erratic manner and have a very difficult time placing their faith and their trust in the actions of others.

As I have discussed earlier, the prevailing thinking is that time heals all wounds, well in this case it is simply not true. These wounds stay with us – and we drag them from relationship to relationship causing havoc, pain and distress.

Signs That You Have a Fearful Avoidant Attachment Relationship and Dating Style.

Because you have a combination of avoidant and anxious relationship and dating attachment styles, you will get a lot of mixed and confusing behaviors and messages.

Relationships and dating are very difficult for adults who have this attachment style because, on one hand, they have the desire to be accepted and to be in a relationship and on the other they have an intense fear of being in a close intimate relationship because they are plagued by an intense anxiety that those who are closest to them will ultimately hurt them in some way.

They have a hard time thinking that their partner will accept and love them just the way they are and will stand by them.

This mentality can evolve into self-sabotaging behavior, leading an adult who is fearful avoidant to leave a relationship sooner than it should have been ended therefore making it a self-fulfilling prophesy.

As you can imagine, dating or relating to a person with a fearful avoidant attachment style is not an easy thing to do.

Imagine participating in a game where you have only a vague understanding of the rules, and that the rules are changing constantly.

As you can see whether a person is avoidant, anxious, or fearful avoidant in relationships or in dating – it can cause a lot of pain and anguish for both parties.

But please know this. When you finally decide to heal your wounds from the past, when you finally decide to do the work to get to the root causes of your unhealthy dating and relationship attachment patterns and behaviors you can, and **you will start picking your relationship partners from the best version of yourself** instead of from a place of loneliness, low-self esteem, damage, neediness, or a need for validation.

You can and you will start communicating from a much more secure and grounded place, instead of a place that's guarded and untrusting and just waiting for the next trigger.

When you heal the wounds of the past and move to a more secure and grounded dating and relationship attachment style, you can finally free yourself from the disempowering limiting beliefs that have been keeping you stuck in a mindset that there are no good men left.

Because trust me when I say this. **Yes, there are good, high-value, masculine men that are available,** and let me show you where they are.

When you heal the wounds of the past and move to a more secure and grounded dating and relationship attachment style, you can start trusting again.

Because trust is the foundation of every great relationship. Without trust, you can never be truly vulnerable with your partner, and without vulnerability, you will never have the deep connection your soul longs for.

When we take the time to heal the wounds from our past, we will become more grounded in all of our relationships. When we are more grounded in who we are, we can and will set better standards and boundaries for ourselves, which leads to partners who will treat us with more respect and where we feel like we have a voice in our relationships.

I only wish I had known about this kind of work when I was 20 years old. I would have saved myself a lot of pain and a lot of misery.

Because whatever you think you are. You will find a way to create it in your life, and you will prove yourself right.

If you have a belief that you are unworthy of love, that you are a "loser," that you are not deserving, that no one will ever love you for you, that you are not good enough, or that there are no good men left. That will ultimately be your experience of the world and how the world experiences you.

Just read all of these negative, disempowering beliefs. How are we ever going to experience real intimacy or deep connection in a relationship with the most AMAZING man of our dreams with all of this going on inside of us?

You will end up pushing away from you what it is that you say you want, or you will end up picking the wrong relationship partners to prove your belief as true, thereby reinforcing it, and this leads to the worst part of self-sabotaging behavior.

Shame, deep shame, and regret.

This leads to an even greater truth. **We cannot expect the world to change the way it shows up for us unless we are prepared to change the way we show up for it.**

YOU need to become the leader in your life and your relationship, the hero in your own life's story, the person who INSPIRES your partner to follow you, to respect your boundaries, and to believe in you.

Leaders take 100% responsibility for how they are showing up in their life, who they are being, and who they are attracted to. They take 100% responsibility to make the necessary changes in themselves to be the best partner for their partner and themselves.

Whereby they make the **MASSIVE internal shift in the intention of the life** that they are living, and the way they communicate and relate to their partner that **becomes "we" focused,** instead of being "me" focused.

And when you make this massive shift in being, your EXPERIENCE with dating, relationships, and with the opposite sex CHANGES because their experience of you changes!

And I need you to know this, this is your not your fault, this is not your parent's fault. This is how we as a society are socialized, and it is passed down from generation to generation.

Many of us wear the mask, the mask that everything is ok – until the next relationship partner, until the next failed relationship, until the next breakup.

Because the biggest mistake I have made in my life was believing the **"well- intentioned" lie that time heals all wounds.**

Not only have I discovered that this is untrue in my own life, but I have also discovered that it is untrue through my work with my clients.

New brain science conclusively proves that there are certain memories that stay with us from childhood and deeply affect how we see ourselves throughout our entire lives.

They are called implicit memories, and they quite literally become the lens through which we see and experience our world and our relationships with others.

Implicit memories **implant themselves deep within our subconscious minds** and serve as a foundation for our belief system.

Proving that our thoughts do NOT create our reality.

Our subconscious beliefs, biases, patterns, habits, and fears **drive our behaviors** and are mostly responsible for actually creating our reality every single moment of the day, and for most of us, we are not even consciously aware of it.

This is why for a lot of people, positive affirmations and a lot of therapies do not work.

Because we need to **clear out our disempowering beliefs and our wounds from the past from the subconscious mind first** before we can ever hope to heal and let go of our unhealthy relationship and dating attachment styles, attitudes, and behaviors!

This is why I say more than likely it's not just counseling that you need, it's healing.

Because over time if you have adopted the belief that you are not good enough, that people cannot be trusted, that you are ultimately powerless to create the life for yourself that you have always wanted or that sooner or later you will be abandoned or hurt by the people that you care about.

That disempowering limiting belief you hold deep down in your subconscious mind will be **subconsciously sabotaging you at a very deep level** beyond your awareness. And that is a very scary thought.

That's why if someone makes you jealous or upset about something, and you have not done the work, you will most likely be triggered and respond in defensiveness or anger.

You can't help yourself. It is your brain on autopilot.

In that moment, your subconscious mind takes over, their pain becomes a mirror for the projection of your pain.

I have also discovered that for the vast majority of us, these deep-seated wounds and beliefs are not something you can heal or let go of by watching another video on YouTube, reading another self-help or relationship book off of Amazon, going on another spiritual retreat, 12 step program, or hoping that they will disappear over time.

I've had clients who have spent thousands upon thousands of dollars and spent years and years of their lives in therapy with little to show for it.

We need to go deeper, deeper than you have ever been, **deeper than you have ever thought possible.**

The process I use for healing and letting go of beliefs that no longer serve us involves **peeling back the layers of the onion** that make up your life's intricate stories and beliefs and then helping you heal, let them go, and essentially "wipe the slate clean" which allows you to reinvent yourself, into the most powerful, confident, joyful, loving version of yourself.

Powerful is the woman who takes the time to invest in herself and do the work, to finally heal the wounds of her past.

Confident is the woman who is comfortable going after what she wants. Showing up, taking up space, no longer needing or looking for validation from others.

Joyful is the woman who truly loves the life she is living.

And loving is the woman who fully embraces her femininity as she radiates warmth in the person whom she is BEING.

This in my opinion is the woman who is absolutely irresistible to men. A woman who is feminine, playful, vulnerable, kind, and sexy.

Healing and "letting go" allow us to drop our triggers, projections, defensiveness, and our deeply held fears of not being good enough that stand in the way of true communication, vulnerability, and deep connection with our partners.

It's time to step up and level up in your life and in who you are being.

I call it an inside-out, life-changing TRANSFORMATION!

I discovered that when you heal and let go of your disempowering, limiting beliefs, your unhealthy relationship patterns, and your wounds from the past.

You can, and you will heal your feelings of loneliness, anxiety, and fear, and **change your life!**

You will feel lighter; many of my clients feel like a huge burden has been lifted off of their shoulders. The best way I can describe it is to imagine you are outside on a warm sunny day, walking in a meadow on the side of a mountain, feeling the sun warm your face and skin—your mind is clear, feeling like anything is possible.

I also know that this work that I will be asking you to do will more than likely be very triggering for you. This work forces you to face who you are truly being in your day-to-day life and who you are being in your dating and your relationship life, and it's not easy.

This work, this journey, is not easy for most people, and that is why most people will never do it.

There are no shortcuts, no videos on YouTube, no book, or free advice in Facebook Groups that will help you make this massive internal shift.

It is a process.

Having so much information available for free online is a dual-edged sword. **It can delude us into thinking we are doing the work when we are not.** This kind of work, this kind of change and transformation - is deep.

That is why we have such a high divorce rate in our society. Divorce rates are even higher for second marriages and higher still for third marriages.

Most people will never do the work to heal the wounds from their past, and to change their internal landscape. They just go from relationship to relationship, convincing themselves that it is the other person who is or was "the problem."

But the reality is that there are millions of other people in life in deeply satisfying, loving relationships.

So, why not you?

Know that everything that you have ever wanted is sitting there waiting for you on the other side of your disempowering limiting beliefs, unhealthy relationship patterns, behaviors, and your painful wounds of the past.

EVERYTHING!

And all it takes is a willingness to do the work and the right person to help you get there.

I want you to know that I have a genuine desire to help others and that I genuinely want you to have what I have. A loving, committed, long-term relationship that will go the distance with a life partner that loves, cherishes, and respects you.

To that end, not only do I want to thank you for supporting me by purchasing this book. I also want to show you my appreciation, by extending a very special offer to you.

Our first 60-minute session together is **payable by donation.**

At the end of our first session, please feel free to donate however much you feel comfortable with and whatever you think our session together was worth to you.

And if you need my help and you genuinely have no money, then that's ok too.

I will tell you this, I care deeply, and I am very good at helping people get clarity in how they are getting in their own way of having and living the kind of life that they say they have always wanted by helping them heal and let go of their disempowering limiting beliefs and their painful wounds of their past.

You will find me compassionate and most importantly, non-judgemental.

I am also on a mission. I am very pro-family and I want to help bring both men and women back together again. I want to help both men and women have better, healthier relationships.

If you have unresolved trauma or a painful wound from the past that is still getting in the way of you having successful relationships with men or with you trusting men.

Please do not hesitate to reach out to me for help.

Because getting the help you need does not have to be overly expensive and it does not need to take a lifetime of therapy!

I also believe in paying it forward. So, if you believe in what I am doing, and you want to help me help even more people, you can pay it forward if you want by donating whatever you can afford to the next person who needs my help.

Book some one-on-one time with me by emailing me:

Kevin@Insideout-Dating-Makeover.ca

Let's use that time for you and I, to connect one on one and to go really deep into what is holding you back from living your best life ever with the most amazing man of your dreams!

Things we can talk about that I can help you with;

Do you have trouble trusting men? Let's talk about where that really comes from and how we can heal that wound.

Are you sick and tired of endless dating, long lonely nights and weekends spent alone, mixed and confusing messages from men, and dating emotionally unavailable or abusive men?

Let's talk about your experiences with men, dating, and relationships and how we can help you rebuild your trust with men again, and then let me help you pinpoint exactly what you are most likely doing wrong, and let me show you the best way to have an amazing relationship with the high-quality man of your dreams!

Are you feeling lonely, anxious, frustrated, or have you had your heart broken one too many times? I have a proven very effective healing methodology for depression, loneliness, relationship breakups and breakdowns, to help you "wipe the slate clean" and to help you to rebuild your life, your relationships with men, and your self-esteem!

Do you have a particular question about dating, men, sex, or relationships that I didn't cover in the book, or do you need more clarity on what I meant or to go deeper into a particular topic?

My jam is helping others! Don't be shy, **book a session with me!**

Have trouble communicating, relating to, or understanding men and need some help? This is what I am good at, and this is what I love to do!

Expert, compassionate, non-judgemental advice is only one phone call away.

You have nothing to lose by booking some time to speak with me, and everything to gain!

Book your call with me today by emailing me:

Kevin@Insideout-Dating-Makeover.ca

And let's get started on your new life!

Manufactured by Amazon.ca
Bolton, ON

32213080R00125